ACCELERATE:
PARENTING TEENAGERS TOWARD ADULTHOOD

How Not to Find Your 25-Year-Old Still Living in Your Basement

Richard Ross

We believe that the Bible has God for its author; salvation for its end; and truth,without
any mixture of error, for its matter and that all Scripture is totally true and trustworthy. To
review LifeWay's doctrinal guideline, please visit *www.lifeway.com/doctrinalguideline*.

Unless otherwise noted, all Scripture references are taken from the New American
Standard Bible®, Copyright © 1960, 1962, 1963, 1968, 1971, 1972, 1973, 1975, 1977,
1995 by the Lockman Foundation. Used by permission. (*www.lockman.org*)

ISBN: 9781430051985
Item number: 005778553

Dewey Decimal Classification Number: 248.83
Subject heading: STUDENTS \ STUDENT MINISTRY \ PARENTING

Printed in the United States of America.

Student Ministry Publishing
LifeWay Resources
One LifeWay Plaza
Nashville, Tennessee 37234-0144

Certain stock imagery © Thinkstock.

CHAPTER 1: FAILING TO LAUNCH

Richard Ross

You someday may conclude your 25-year-old is not an adult.

The majority of people between the ages of 18 and 25 do not see the world in adult ways. They know they are not teenagers, but they also sense they are not adults.

Parents, extended family, schoolteachers, church leaders, and other significant adults in their lives had the best of intentions. But many did not give them the modeling, training, and experiences that would have accelerated their development toward adulthood.

The majority of those 18–25:

- Do not have a clear vocational focus or the drive to move forward vocationally.

- Do not feel motivated to achieve independence in their finances or life situation.

- Do not feel ready to accept the lifetime commitments marriage entails.

- Do not feel ready to parent.

- Do not like to delay gratification for a greater good.

- Do not like to work hard for long hours at uninteresting tasks to achieve a goal.

For many believers this age, their faith is an underdeveloped, "adolescent" faith. Most set this weak faith aside during adulthood. Thus, most are not fulfilling their unique calling and mission on earth and not bringing glory to God.

All that is true, but the focus of this book is not on the past or present. It is on the future. With the wisdom and power of the Holy Spirit, parents and other significant adults can begin to rear teenagers in fresh, new ways. The result may well be high school graduates on their way to adulthood, deeply in love with Christ, and wanting nothing more than His glory.

Developmental psychologist J. J. Arnett has identified and labeled a new life stage, one that developed only in the past 50 years. He calls the period from age 18 to 25 Emerging Adulthood.[1] His research suggests these are people who have left their teenage years, but they have not become adults. They know they are in an in-between period of life. For the first time in history, people in their younger twenties may not be adults.

Sex and Marriage

Arnett suggests that one of the primary reasons for the development of this life stage was the sexual revolution of the 1960s. A shift in moral beliefs and the invention of the birth control pill prompted large numbers of people to separate sex from marriage.

Now, 50 years later, high school graduates who are sexually active are less inclined toward marriage and parenting. Some describe sex as similar to shaking hands. They move from partner to partner with almost no commitment. Others move in together. Over two-thirds of young Americans now cohabit before marriage.

Work Ethic

This generation also has a strong focus on self. Child-rearing "experts" told their parents that the self-esteem of children is fragile. They advocated parenting approaches that made children the center of the family and convinced each one that "I am very, very special."

At the same time, growing financial prosperity has meant children and teenagers no longer have to work in order for a family to survive. Well-meaning parents have released their offspring from work inside or outside the home as a loving gift.

High school graduates who feel special and who never developed a strong work ethic tend to approach employment with this sentiment: "I deserve to do only work that is meaningful and rewarding to me— and that offers growth potential so I can continue doing only those things I want to do." But, given their lack of skills and training, those 18–25 tend to find only hourly jobs that are somewhat menial and not "meaningful." Their frustration with such positions causes them to change jobs frequently. On average they change positions seven times between the ages of 20 and 29.[2]

Changing romantic partners often, changing jobs often, and thus moving often gives those in this age range a sense of instability. This uncertainty also causes them to sense they are not adults.

Brain Development

Sometimes they think in ways similar to teenagers because a region of their brain (the prefrontal cortex) is underdeveloped. This region is the thinking and controlling center of the mind. Their brain is underdeveloped because they failed to move through challenging, stimulating, adult-like experiences during the years of 13–18.

The newest brain research demonstrates that real-world, adult-like experiences accelerate the development of the brain.[3] Today, without those experiences, the mind still works in "adolescent" ways through the mid-20s.

Surrounded by Peers

Research by Tim Elmore reveals that teenagers today spend about 60 hours a week with peers and about 16 hours with adults.[4] For most of human history, the reverse of this was true.

Through the centuries, children 4 and older spent most of their time performing chores. They learned to do adult-like tasks by working side by side with adults. By the time they became teenagers, the young were thinking and acting in adult ways because they had been observing and relating to adults all day every day most of their lives.

Today, teenagers spend the vast majority of their time with people their own age. They still observe and imitate the people around them, but those people no longer are adults. No one should be surprised that high school graduates, who just spent six years imitating one another, are not ready to function as adults.

Personal Faith

The National Study of Youth and Religion sent shock waves through the youth ministry world. This careful study discovered that the faith of most church teenagers could be described as moralistic therapeutic deism.[5] The core tenets of this belief system are:

- God exists and He is nice.

- He is not relevant to my daily life, with one exception.

- Any time I have a need, He quickly shows up and takes care of that need.

- Then He goes back to being distant and irrelevant.

The faith that characterizes most church teenagers is almost entirely me centered. And it is a "faith" that usually crumbles after high school. Between 40 and 60 percent of active church youth fail to walk in faith and stay connected to the church in adulthood.[6]

This means most people 18 to 25:

- are not prepared to walk in faith all their lives,

- do not live in intimate relationship with Christ,

- do not value the glory of God above all things,

- do not embrace a love relationship with the local church,

- are not committed to completing the Great Commission— locally and globally, and

- do not stand ready to live—or die if so called—to see Christ's kingdom come on earth.

According to researcher David Kinnaman: "The next generation is caught between two possible destinies—one moored by the power and depth of the Jesus-centered gospel and one anchored to a cheap, Americanized version of the historic faith that will snap at the slightest puff of wind."[7]

Parenting Styles

Most of the parents in the church have made their children one of their highest priorities. Tim Elmore says, "I have not seen a more engaged batch of parents since I began working with students more than thirty years ago."[8]

Those who parented current emerging adults had the very best of intentions. They wanted nothing more than the well-being of their children. However, at times they listened to ill-informed "experts," and other times they were influenced by trends in the culture.

Some became "helicopter" parents. Elmore defines these parents as "the ones who hover over their kids, making sure they get every imaginable advantage and are protected from every imaginable danger.

. . . [They] don't allow their kids the privilege of learning to fail and persevere. They prefer to prepare the path for the child instead of the child for the path."[9]

According to researcher Chris Segrin, "One of the apparent consequences of parents attempting to solve all of their children's problems and to assume responsibility for their child's well-being well into adulthood is that the child never develops a strong belief in his or her own ability to solve problems and achieve goals."[10] Marriage and family researcher Stephenie Lievense adds, "Adult children who have never been allowed to really fail and then learn from those failures aren't able to handle the inevitable blunders of adulthood."[11]

Elmore summarizes the issue by saying, "Our message to (teenagers) has been more about safety and maintenance than about adventure and calling. We have been protecting them rather than preparing them and coddling them instead of calling them out—challenging them to seize opportunities and make a significant contribution."[12]

What do teenagers need instead of helicopter parents? As they mature they need proportionate autonomy and responsibility.

1. "Autonomy: the ability to act independently, with freedom and access to resources.

2. "Responsibility: the ability to be accountable and handle tasks in a dependable way.

"[Teenagers] should experience simultaneous freedom and autonomy in parallel with their ability to assume responsibility. There should be limited exposure to input they aren't yet ready to handle, but they should be encouraged to take increasing responsibility for themselves as they grow. The young adult emerges as one who has risen to the challenges because the standard was set by a caring adult."[13]

Epstein reports what happens when parents appropriately raise the bar with their offspring. The teenagers almost always rise to meet those expectations.[14]

Elmore says it this way: "What adolescents need are adults . . . who make appropriate demands and set appropriate standards for them in a responsive environment of belief and concern. In short, they need adults to display a balance of two characteristics—they need them to be both responsive and demanding:

1. "Responsive—to display acceptance, support, and patience; to be attentive to them

2. "Demanding—to establish standards and hold them accountable to those standards"[15]

Challenge, appropriate risk, freedom to fail, increasing autonomy, and clear expectations accelerate teenagers toward full adulthood—if all of that is happening in an atmosphere of unconditional love and support. Parents who move in these directions may find fewer 25-year- olds living in their basement.

The Future

Today, people 18–25 do not see themselves as adults, and they know they are not prepared for adult roles. Spiritually, socially, and emotionally, they are underdeveloped. Even regions of their brains are underdeveloped.

As a parent, you stand at a crossroads. If you repeat the parenting approaches of the past, your children may well become 20-somethings similar to those today—living in a never, never land between the teenage years and adulthood.

Or you can seek the wisdom of the Holy Spirit and think new thoughts. You can link arms with church leaders and other significant adults and begin to parent in fresh new ways. Those fresh approaches are the focus of this book. Soon you may see your own high school graduates well on their way to adulthood, deeply in love with Christ, and wanting nothing more than His glory.

CHAPTER 2: RECALLING THE AMAZING POTENTIAL SEEN IN PAST GENERATIONS

Johnny L. Derouen

Your teenager has the amazing potential seen in past generations of those that age.

> Let no one look down on your youthfulness, but rather
> in speech, conduct, love, faith and purity, show yourself
> an example of those who believe (1 Tim. 4:12).

At 17, your great-grandfather likely plowed all day behind a mule and then went home to help with the baby. Your great-grandmother worked just as hard and just as competently. At 16 she washed clothes by hand with soap she had made, cooked from a fire she had built, roasted chickens she raised herself, took care of the children, planted her own garden, and still had time to care for her husband. Both performed well in their roles because adults had invested years preparing them for just that.

You may wonder whether adolescence is just an artificial extension of childhood. You probably have seen research that suggests teenagers today, unlike their ancestors, lack responsibility, are addicted to online gaming and pornography, and generally are out of sync with the adult world. This is seen in the way teenagers relate to school, romantic relationships, long-term employment, and their relationship with Jesus Christ. Many become young adults who have a difficult time applying past lessons to future problems, delaying gratification to achieve a greater goal, setting long-term objectives, and working before playing.

But have teenagers always seemed irresponsible, immature, and aimless? Taking a trip back in history and recalling what your ancestors were like as teenagers may give you a startling and encouraging surprise. What teenagers can do and have done can change how you view raising responsible teenagers in today's world. Rather than sentencing teenagers to immaturity and prolonged adolescence, God designed them to do so much more than you may have considered.

The Terms Teenager and Adolescence

The first commonly used name representing those aged 13–19 was the word *teen*, coined in 1818. *Teener*, followed in 1894. The term *teenager* first was used in 1941 as a more "mature" sounding substitute for *teener*.[1]

The word *adolescence*, Latin for *adolescere* (to grow up), came into being in the 1400s. It was not commonly used to represent an age grouping until the early 1900s, through the impact of G. Stanley Hall's book, *Adolescence*.[2]

Many developments led the culture to perceive a new age group. Adolescence, as a stage of life, was the creation of modern industrialization, child labor laws, school systems, and other factors that moved into high gear between 1880 and 1920.[3]

For the first time in human history, culture artificially extended childhood well past puberty. One perspective, called the inventionist view, would say adolescence was a social and historical creation. During this period of the 1800s and early 1900s, special laws were enacted that restricted teenage options, encouraged dependence, and caused a decline in apprenticeships.

> Simply put, youth and youth culture were invented because we needed them. With the shift from manual labor to machines and the emergence of a professional class requiring prolonged education, a new stage of life was defined for teenagers. Instead of learning a trade, running the farm or working in a factory, teenagers were expected—no required—to go to school. Instead of getting married and having children, teenagers were encouraged to (stay in school, remain in the teenage world) and abstain from or practice safe sex (put off marriage until later).[4]

For most of human history, especially before 1880, children and teenagers worked side by side with parents and adults as soon as they were able. After the 1880s, new laws and cultural practices began to separate teenagers from adults. This separation led to:

1. Youth separated from significant adult role models and social roles in the community. The available roles left to them were limited to education, consumption, and peer relationships.

2. Youth separated from networks of care in the local community.

This would include families and other adult groups. Teenagers now are largely connected to and by peer relationships with little adult involvement.

3. Youth losing attention on the common good. Teenagers are seduced by a mass-mediated culture to focus on stuff, celebrity, and the posh lifestyle.

4. Youth segregated within faith communities, including services and buildings designed just for them. They have little time to connect with adults other than youth workers.

5. Youth not expected to fully attend to the call of God upon their lives. Youth feeling they do not have any real power to shape a better world. Youth doubting that God may actually call them to something greater than themselves. Youth not challenged to explore their abilities and then respond to God's call to live and die for Him.

6. Youth left to themselves, where their need for security and the desire for consumption drives their lifestyle and vocational choices.[5]

Separation of work and home, age-graded schools, urbanization, the appearance of youth groups such as Boy/Girl Scouts, YMCA/YWCA, age-graded church ministries, and educators writing on adolescence added to this new age development. This expanded what is known as the youth years. A century later the MacArthur Foundation now suggests that adolescence officially ends at 34 years of age.[6]

Teenage Ancestors

Throughout most of human history, your ancestors began to marry and produce children shortly after puberty. This was good since life spans were shorter in earlier ages.[7] These young ancestors must have been capable of providing for their offspring, defending their family from predators, cooperating with other humans, and functioning fully as adults. If not, their young would not have survived, and the human race would have ended. The fact that people still are here suggests that most teenagers are far more capable than we sometimes think.

Yet it appears adults today have lost sight of the potential of teenagers. Seldom are teenagers allowed important roles in society, especially in the church. Teenagers sometimes become leaders among their peers, but that is all.

According to the 2012 U.S. Census, the average age of first-time marriage for males is 28.6 and for females, 26.6. This appears to have slowed down the taking of responsibility.

For most of human history, children learning and working alongside parents and other adults transitioned to adulthood by their early to late teens. Young people married soon after puberty and set up independent households.

The historical discussion that follows reveals that teenagers can have valuable roles in adult society. A quick glance back into the teenage past may provide a better understand of the capability of the young.

Teenagers in the Biblical Period

Teenagers in the Bible usually functioned fully as adults. They played important roles in adult society. They were kings, reformers, warriors, leaders, prophets, officials, heroes, scholars, and parents. The following facts reveal the value of teenagers in biblical times:

1. The mother of Jesus was, in all probability, a young teenager. Given the marriage practices of the day, most girls were married and had children by age 13 or 14.[8]

2. Scripture hints that 11 of the 12 disciples were probably teenagers. (Matthew 17 may suggest only Peter and Jesus owed the temple tax, due from those 21 and older, and thus excluding the other 11 apostles).[9]

3. There is no period of adolescence in the Bible.

4. There are only two age restrictions in the Old Testament. One had to be 20 to be drafted (forced to fight) in the military (although there are no restrictions for fighting at younger ages), to be counted in the census, to be obligated to serve in the temple as a Levite, to be required to give offerings to God, and to be required to pay taxes. Twenty-five was the age required to work in the tent of meetings (Num. 8:24).

5. There are no age restrictions in the New Testament.

6. It appears that age was not a factor as much as responsibility, faith in God, respect, and obedience. One's birthright, boldness, ability, and being in

the right place at the right time (with a lot of help from God!) carried more weight in the Bible and ancient times than age. The young were expected to rise up and be responsible.

7. Jesus was in the temple teaching and discussing Scripture at age 12. What an example! (Luke 2:41–47).

8. Some of the amazing teenagers in the Bible were King Uzziah, King Josiah, King David, Daniel, Joseph, Samuel, Samson, and Esther.

9. Traditional Jewish culture considers one to become a functioning adult, begin to observe the mitzvot (Jewish commandments/rituals), and become a fully functioning part of the community around age 12 or 13. Viewing someone at age 13 as adult and a fully functioning part of the community was first mentioned in 180 AD in the Pirkei Avot (Ethics of Fathers) of the Talmud.

10. The observance of the Bar and Bat Mitzvah also gave weight to early adulthood. The Bar Mitzvah for boys was first celebrated in the Middle Ages, and the Bat Mitzvah for girls was first celebrated in the U.S. in 1922.[10]

Teenagers in the Ancient World

1. Counselors/advisors in ancient Greco-Roman principalities could be as young as four. These positions primarily were ceremonial, as they were being groomed to be full-fledged advisors by age 17. They were no longer considered as children but as apprentice adults.[11]

2. Young people were mentored and groomed as apprentice adults for political offices, business leadership, and more as early as childhood and early puberty.

3. Adolescence, as we know it, did not exist in the ancient world. Many historians of childhood have pointed out that young people today are much more sheltered than they were before the industrial age and less likely to be integrated into adult society until much older. The historical record reveals this early integration to adulthood and the lack of tumult that resulted.[12] Jean Liedloff concluded from her studies with other youth cultures that it is a mistake to isolate and shelter teenagers from adult society.[13]

Teenage Cognitive Abilities

1. Studies show that cognitive abilities are, more or less, fully developed soon after puberty.[21]

2. Reasoning ability, intelligence, and memory functions peak in the mid teen years.[22]

3. Cognitive skills and decision-making skills are equal to that of adults for early and mid-teens.[23]

4. Studies show that the teen brain is a reflection of teen problems and not their cause. The teen brain is not the culprit; society is.[24]

5. Brain volume peaks at around age 14, shrinks 25 percent a few years after puberty, and continues shrinking throughout the lifespan.[25]

6. Most teenagers, with parental and adult help, are capable of adult moral reasoning.[26]

7. Three of the most widely used IQ tests, WCIS, WAIS, and Raven's "Progressive Matrices" (the predecessor of culture free, nonverbal IQ tests), indicate that IQ peaks at 15.5–16 years.[27]

Teenagers Today

Teenagers today are more sheltered than they were before the dawn of the Industrial Age, 1880–1920. There is danger to teenagers when parents infantilize and disempower teens or do not teach them and give them responsibilities. You can make life hard for your teenagers by trying to make it easy for them. History and research tend to point to the fact that teenagers are capable but not challenged, taught, and expected to take on responsibility. On the other hand:

1. What if teenagers were led, expected, and allowed to take on responsibility at home and at church, alongside adults?

2.   What if teenagers were taught how to handle, study, and teach the Bible and not just taught the Bible?

3.   What if training before and after rites of passage led children to take on more adult roles with responsibilities?

New Testament professor David A. Black concludes: "It is my conviction that the social theory of adolescence undermines both the Christian understanding of human nature and the way in which Christians analyze moral thought. It underscores the modern disinclination to treat a person as responsible for his or her actions. When we assert the 'fact' that teenagers are to act like children rather than adults, it becomes a self-fulfilling prophecy."[28]

Remarkable Teenagers

1.   As a teenager in Fort Worth, Austin Adkins began a campus club at his high school with some of his friends. This ministry led scores of students to walk with and honor Jesus Christ, impacting the school in many ways. Many of these students later entered vocational ministry.

2.   Florrie Evans was an eighth-grade girl in New Quay, Cardiganshire, Wales. Many historians believe God used her courage and faith to spark the worldwide spiritual awakening that swept the world in 1904–1906, with millions coming to know Jesus Christ.

3.   In 1971, two high school siblings in Lake Charles, Louisiana, Jon and Sandi Schellack, began to pray for God to move in LaGrange Senior High School. They met most mornings at 6:30 AM to pray. After three months of prayer, a spiritual awakening occurred that lasted for one and a half years, resulting in hundreds of students coming to know and follow Jesus Christ. Many followed God's call into vocational ministry, including the author of this chapter.

4.   After graduating from high school in New Jersey, Maggie Doyne went on a backpacking trip in Asia. She was so moved by the many orphans she met in Nepal that she decided to stay and care for them. She used her savings to buy an acre of land and built an orphanage. She dedicated her life to care for orphans. She currently cares for 24 orphans and has helped find

families to adopt more than seven hundred more. She now is planning to build a school to educate her orphans.

5. Before Alexa Sankary's close friend died from neuroblastoma, he asked her to find a cure. She planned two three-mile walkathons in 2008 and 2009, raising a total of $56,000 for neuroblastoma research. She was chosen by Cook Children's Medical Center, Fort Worth, Texas, as the first youth philanthropist to receive its highest honor. As he presented the award, the hospital vice president said, "The act of philanthropy is not reserved for those of advanced age or affluence."

6. Twenty-five high school seniors, attending summer camp with Travis Avenue Baptist Church in Fort Worth, believed God wanted to do something special in the summer of 1997. They gave up their free time in the afternoon and prayed for two hours each day for God to move. On Thursday night of that week, God came in power. Scores of students came to know Christ. Many others restored broken relationships with their parents and fellow students, let go of things in their lives that were destructive to them, made specific plans to reach their campuses for Christ, and requested prayers for following God's call on their lives. The revival followed these students back to Fort Worth and spread. The moving of God stayed fresh for a number of years afterward as these teenagers planned, on their own, many ways to make the name of Jesus known to their friends.

7. Students in Perrin, a small town in north Texas, have taken God at His Word and are meeting together to pray for God to use them and their town to bring about a spiritual awakening.

8. Mother Teresa of Calcutta started her work at age 19.

9. Louis Braille completed the Braille System at age 16.

10. Stan Lee (Stanley Leiber) made his comic book debut with *Captain America Foils the Traitor's Revenge* at age 17 and became an editor in chief at age 18.

11. S. E. Hinton wrote the novel *The Outsiders* at age 16.

12. Gaspard Monge originated differential and descriptive geometry at 16.

13. Karl Gauss invented the method of "least squares" at 18. 14. Mary Shelley wrote *Frankenstein* at 18.

15. Samuel Colt built his first model for the Colt revolver, by designing a "pepperbox gun" with a cylinder that rotated when the trigger was cocked, at 16.

16. George Parker created his first board game, Banking, and founded Parker Brothers Board Game Company at age 16 in 1883.

17. Cassie Bernall stood for her faith at gunpoint and died at age 17 during the Columbine High School massacre.

18. Bill Gates started Microsoft at age 19.

19. At 17, John Wesley developed the faith and convictions that would launch the Methodist movement.

20. Blaise Paschal invented the calculator at age 18 and his theory on conic sections at age 16.

21. Zach Hunter launched the modern initiative to set slaves free at 15.

22. Mark Zuckerberg started Facebook at 19.

Never underestimate what God can do through teenagers and what they are capable of when challenged and prepared.

Human beings have the capacity increasingly to think and act in adult-like ways through the teenage years:

- If their brains have received proper stimulation.

- If they have learned adult critical thinking.

- If they have learned knowledge and roles through observation and formal instruction from parents and other adults.

Teenagers are capable of making great contributions to society and the cause of Jesus Christ. Currently they have few ways of being heard and making those contributions.

If you have a fresh walk with Jesus and model and teach adult responsibility to your children, you likely will see them walk responsibly into their young adult years. They likely will have wisdom and will make a major impact for Jesus Christ. What an opportunity you have to raise up a generation of responsible adults who love Jesus Christ and desire to make his name known and honored around the world (see Prov. 3:5–6 and Ps. 25:14).

The ultimate call is not to be a super-Christian, superparent, biblical expert, or theological genius. The highest calling is found in Deuteronomy 6:5. You are called to love God with all of your heart, soul, and might. You are to follow Him, to seek Him, and to be transparent so your faith shows. Second Corinthians 7:1 calls you to do all you do out of reference for God.

Then you will, in the power of the Spirit, create in your children a love for Jesus. That love will give them a hunger to know and follow Him. You will be used of God to build responsibility, depth, and autonomy in your children, accelerating them toward adulthood.

"The teenager is a recent idea that may not deserve to be an eternal one."[29]

CHAPTER 3: SEEING A FRESH VISION FOR YOUR TEENAGER

Richard Ross

You someday may conclude your 25-year-old is an adult, emotionally and spiritually.

Small changes in the home and church will not be adequate to create a generation of high school graduates who are far more mature, far more ready to take on adult roles, and far more ready to join King Jesus in bringing His kingdom on earth. Before considering new ways to accelerate growth, you need to consider,

> "Am I ready to declare my independence from
> what is average—in order to launch a generation
> that is mature and looks a lot like Jesus?"

God designed humankind before the foundation of the world. That included designing every facet of people who would move through the ages of 12–18. Observing such people in the biblical period and in early centuries reveals that God chose to build amazing potential in that age group.

Those same spiritual, mental, emotional, and social potentials exist within teenagers today. If you and other parents respond to those teenagers in new ways, future young adults again can fulfill the possibilities they carry within them.

In just a few years, imagine launching 18-year-olds:

- Who live for the glory of God.
- Who invite the Spirit to empower them to enjoy and order life under the supreme lordship of High King Jesus.
- Who have a deep understanding of the gospel.
- Who know the depth of the Father's love toward them and show lifetime gratitude for the grace that has been extended to them.

- Who invite Christ to live His powerful life through them.

- Who join Him in making disciples among all peoples.

- Who have an identity and a purpose on earth anchored in who they are in Christ.

- Who love others more than they love themselves.

- Who exhibit biblical servanthood and a willingness to sacrifice for others.

- Who have a strong work ethic.

- Who are willing to delay gratification.

- Who are willing to do the mundane for hours to accomplish a goal.

- Who appreciate all the sacrifices parents have made, but now are ready to get on with their lives.

- Who have goals and know how to move toward those goals.

- Who move toward lifetime marriages if God should so lead.

- Who understand pregnancy, childbirth, and the care of babies.

- Who are prepared to parent if God should allow.

- Who know, understand, and can state their faith.

- Who experience the spiritual disciplines in mature ways.

- Who can defend their faith.

- Who can share their faith.

- Who have a uniquely biblical worldview.

- Who feed themselves spiritually and take initiative for their own spiritual growth through the Spirit.

- Who know how to lead and how to follow at church.

- Who enjoy relationships and kingdom service with all the generations at church.

- Who know how to find the will of God.

- Who join Christ in changing the world.

- Who go out to reach the last unreached people groups on the earth.

- Who have sails raised to spark revival in the church.

- Who live and, if called on, die for the glory of God.

- Who know how to care for their home, transportation, possessions, and health.

- Who know how to make wise decisions about finances.

- Who know how to form and sustain adult friendships.
- Who know the principles for succeeding in any vocation.
- Who know how to succeed in college or in whatever life preparation God ordains.

Living Life Differently

Secular people tell you lots of things you probably don't believe. Things similar to:

- Inconvenient babies can be swept away before birth.
- We are all on different paths, but everyone will get to heaven.

Here are some other things secular people might want you to believe:

- We can continue to parent the way most have in the past, but we magically can expect our offspring to turn out differently.
- It's OK to be busy doing good things even if they are not the best things.
- When it comes to kids, the primary measures of success are wealth, beauty, power, and fame.

As noted earlier, Christian parents must ask, "Am I ready to declare my independence from what is common in the culture—in order to launch a generation that is mature and looks a lot like Jesus?" You prayerfully must consider major changes. You can choose to live and lead in ways that will make you very different from both the secular culture and, at times, even the prevailing church culture.

Tim Elmore, president of Growing Leaders, says it this way: "Mature, healthy people live by a set of values and principles. They don't merely *react* to whatever the culture is doing around them. They *act* based on who they genuinely are."[1]

You might decide your evenings and weekends are about to become very different from the other families in your neighborhood. Consider these scenarios:

Neighbor: Yea, my boy's really something. He played three different sports last Saturday, and he was on the winning team all three times. What did your boy do?"

Wise Parent: He played a soccer game early, and then he volunteered at the hospital the rest of the day. He and I think experiences like these will give him a leg up in the medical field someday.

* * * * *

Jogging Partner: Sometimes I think about spending some time with my kids in the evening—you know, one-on-one. But can I be honest? When I finally get home, I'm so tired all I want to do is hold that remote and later check my Facebook. Pushing hard to get us in that new gated community just about takes all I have.

Wise Parent: I'm moving pretty fast to keep food on the table myself. But sometimes I like to picture myself running on batteries. I make decisions about my job and my other commitments with my kids in mind. I want to come home with enough charge in the batteries that I can give them what they need to prosper as adult followers of Jesus.

* * * * *

Church Member: Did you see *Modern Messed-Up Family* on TV last night? It was hilarious.

Wise Parent: Missed it. I did see my favorite show early, but then I spent some time teaching my daughter how to buy and finance a home. She graduates from high school next year, and we want her to know how to do adult things when she does.

* * * * *

Friend at Work: That college daughter of mine has been texting me about some boy she thinks she loves. I told her to cool it. In fact, I told her if she gets married during college, we will cut her off financially. She needs to graduate and make some good money before she starts thinking about a wedding.

Wise Parent: I wouldn't want my college daughter flippantly getting married either. But if she finds God's person and God's leadership—and the two of them want to continue their education as husband and wife—then we are ready to help with her tuition the way we always planned.

* * * * *

Church Parent: Man, I love that new youth pastor. He can hold those kids spellbound when he speaks.

Wise Parent: I love him too. What I appreciate most is the training he's given me. Now I'm able to show my son how to interpret any passage of Scripture on his own. Someday soon he may use those skills to prepare dorm Bible studies and then to disciple my grandchildren.

* * * * *

Boss: Boy did we have drama last night. My daughter was some kind of unhappy that I missed her dance recital. She doesn't realize what it takes here to get the corner office. I decided awhile back I was ready to run with the big dogs. She ought to appreciate what I'm able to buy the family instead of whining about my missing a couple of things.

Wise Parent: I want to be valuable to our company too. You've probably noticed I give 100 percent during regular work hours. But then I head to the house to pursue another dream. What I really want is to see my kids leave home with a clear purpose, knowing how to think and act as adults, ready to build a great home, and wanting to join Christ is changing the world.

* * * * *

The core issue is this: Teenagers are on earth to live in a grace-drenched love relationship with God and to glorify Him as they join Christ in fulfilling their mission on earth. You are on earth for exactly the same purpose. You will fulfill a major part of your purpose by rearing children who fulfill theirs. Such cosmic issues call for radical changes in how you and your teenagers spend time—especially related to media, extracurricular activities, and extended hours at work.

Media

Parents often say, "We're moving too fast to see much TV. I'm lucky if I get a minute or two to flip that remote." Parents who make such statements really do think they are telling the truth. What they may not realize is that those minutes "flipping the remote" add up.

The fact of the matter is that the parents of teenagers watch an average of just over three hours of TV a night.[2] For many that may mean two favorite shows plus local and national news.

Here is a radical question. What if you watched a total of two hours of TV an evening? That might mean two favorite shows, or it might mean a favorite show plus local and national news. Would two hours of TV give you time to physically rest and mentally relax? If you could look forward to more entertainment time Friday and Saturday evenings, would two hours be adequate Monday through Thursday?

Moving from three hours to two hours of TV might open up a new hour to connect with offspring. That hour might make a major difference in the future of a teenager.

You may prefer social networking and other online activities over TV, but the principle remains the same. Making a conscious decision to limit total media consumption can give you new minutes to invest in your children.

Extracurricular Activities for Teenagers

Extracurricular activities for children and teenagers can have value. Involvement in such activities can:

- Teach teamwork.

- Teach tenacity and the importance of keeping commitments.

- Provide an alternative to bad behavior by unsupervised kids.

- Instill a desire for excellence.

- Hone a gift or skill.

- Create friendships with peers and adult leaders.

- Provide joy and enhanced self-esteem from genuine accomplishments.

Similar to extracurricular activities, dark chocolate has several positive benefits. The flavonoids in dark chocolate can improve heart health, blood pressure, reduce LDL "bad" cholesterol, and increase blood flow to the brain. Young people who enjoy about one ounce of dark chocolate (six Hersey's Kisses) a day experience health benefits and almost no negatives.[3]

On the other hand, parents who allow children to eat a pound of chocolate a day set their kids up for all kinds of health problems. Too much of almost anything is not going to turn out well.

One well-chosen extracurricular activity may help you rear a child who is prepared for adulthood and who wants to join Christ in changing the world. But as you add activities, at some point an "ounce" becomes a "pound," and the sum total of those activities is harming more than helping. Even if each activity is mostly positive, the sum total can lead to teenagers who are distant from the family, ill prepared for the adult world, and stunted spiritually.

Imagine your daughter is on a soccer team and you value what she is learning from that experience. Now she is asking to add dance classes to her life. Several friends are taking dance, and she thinks it would be fun. As you consider whether to approve this addition, you might ask questions such as:

1. Do we pretty consistently get four or five family dinners a week, where we can relax, tell the stories of the day, and enjoy one another? If so, will a new activity place that at risk? If we already get too-few dinners together, should we be simplifying rather than making life more complicated?

2. Do we presently have time each week for about three half- hour conversations about faith and about preparation for adulthood? If so, will a new activity place that at risk? If we cannot find time for relaxed talks today, should we reduce activity rather than add activity?

3. At present, do we have big blocks of time I can use to teach my daughter a strong work ethic and give her experiences in fields that may lead to a lifetime vocation? If so, could a new activity replace work that has lifetime value with something that will not matter that much in adulthood? If my daughter has no hours at present to work part-time or to try out various vocations, what might we take off her schedule rather than add to it?

Four-year-olds sincerely believe they can play safely with butcher knives. Ten-year-olds sincerely believe they should climb over the balcony guardrail at the top of a tall building. Teenagers sincerely believe they should be in band, baseball, one-act play, and debate all at the same time. In all three cases parents need to be the parents. You make decisions for your children at certain stages when they are not developmentally prepared to make those decisions all alone.

If you choose to limit activities in order to build your teenager into a great adult, then each activity must be chosen with prayer and careful thought. As with every other decision related to parenting, the primary question always is, What is my ultimate goal for this child?

The following questions also can help you choose activities:

1. Am I certain I'm interested in this activity for the benefit of my child and not because I have a need to relive part of my life through him or her?

2. Am I certain I'm interested in this activity for the benefit of my child and not because I want to use it to reduce college expenses through scholarships?

3. Will the leader of this activity respect and support our family's commitment to corporate worship on Sunday mornings?

4. Does the leader of this activity seem to require extreme numbers of extra practices—not to benefit the participants but to climb up the ladder to better paying positions?

5. Do those who lead and administer this activity at every level seem to view it as a tool to build great young people and not as an end itself?

Extended Hours at Work

Your clear goals for parenting will cause you to approach media and extracurricular activity differently from the neighbors. And you will evaluate your hours at work in ways that differ from the culture.

Some parents have no latitude related to hours at work. For example, a young widow with two preschoolers may have no alternative but to work long hours to keep food on the table. Parents in unique situations who make great sacrifices to provide for their children are heroes. Christ knows all the details of such situations, and Scripture says He becomes personally involved in meeting the extra needs there.

Other parents have the privilege of making choices about extending hours of work. Almost every parent who works extended hours says he or she is doing so to provide economic advantages and support for the family. That may not always be true.

Consider the following questions:

1. Is it possible I still am trying to get my earthly father's blessing? After all these years, am I hoping I will achieve something at work that finally will cause him to say he is proud of me?

2. Is it possible I never have found my true identity in who I am in Christ? Am I hoping work success finally will cause me to believe I am a worthy person?

3. Is it possible I enjoy being placed on a pedestal at work, and so I want to stay there as many hours a day as I can?

4. Is it possible I prefer and choose the neat and tidy atmosphere at work over the normal chaos and stress of family life?

5. Is it possible I see vocational success as the primary point of life and thus worthy of sacrifice in every other part of life?

Some parents work lots of overtime for a much simpler reason. They really do believe that giving more economic advantages to their children is the most loving thing they can do. Such motives are admirable, but they may be misguided.

To have warm, relational heart connections with mom and dad, teenagers need blocks of time with parents. To be discipled at home and thus transformed into the image of Christ, teenagers need blocks of time with parents. To experience worship as a family, teenagers need blocks of time with parents. To have rich conversations about adult roles and adult life, teenagers need blocks of time with parents.

Teenagers who get to live in the best neighborhoods but are distant from parents are the losers. Teenagers who attend the top private schools but see mom and dad only in passing are the losers. Teenagers who vacation in the best resorts but have broken heart connections with parents are the losers. Teenagers given anything by parents who chose extra work over a relationship with their children are the losers.

Few of those in hospice wish they had spent more time at work. They almost all wish they had spent more time with family.

Conclusion

As you read the next seven chapters, you can think new ways or old ways. When this book suggests taking 30 minutes to teach your son about taxes or caring for babies, you can respond with:

Old Thinking: We don't have five extra minutes in an evening, so a half hour is ridiculous.

New Thinking: Now that my son is only on one league, I think we can find the 30 minutes to get him ready to be an adult.

When this book suggests gathering your family for relaxed prayer and conversations about faith, you can respond with:

Old Thinking: We cannot all get in the same room at the same time because we are never in the same house at the same time.

New Thinking: Since everyone now is making it to dinner on time, I think we can get in some prayer, Scripture, and conversations before we push back from the table.

You are on planet Earth to live in a grace-drenched love relationship with Christ and to glorify Him as you complete your mission and purpose on Earth. You fulfill a major part of that purpose by rearing children who also love God and fulfill their unique purpose. Nothing is more important. If you agree, you will make significant changes in schedules and lifestyles in order to see offspring who look a lot like Jesus and who fully are prepared for adult life.

CHAPTER 4: LAUNCHING TEENAGERS TOWARD ADULTHOOD THROUGH RITES OF PASSAGE

Kyle Crowell

You can accelerate your teenager toward adulthood through a memorable journey and ceremony.

Need for Rites of Passage

The endgame of parenting is adulthood. But a clear definition of *adulthood* can be hard to come by. Just think about it. How would you define *adulthood*? When did you become an adult?

An informal survey of middle school, high school, and college students revealed the confusion that exists within the U.S. regarding adulthood.

Here is how they answered the question, When are you an adult?

- When you experience puberty.
- When you can swear and not get in trouble.
- When you start dating.
- When you can drive a car.
- When you have sex.
- When you smoke your first cigarette.
- When you graduate high school.
- When you turn 18 years old.
- When you can vote.
- When you can be drafted for military service.
- When you legally can drink.
- When you graduate college.
- When you get married.
- When you have a child.

- When you buy a house.
- When you have a full-time job.

As you look at an item on the list, you may think to yourself, *Doing that doesn't make you an adult.* You might also notice that some of these "milestones of adulthood" can happen to the very young or to immature people. Teenagers are getting mixed messages all around them.[1]

Here is an example that reveals some of the mixed messages culture sends students about adulthood: The starting linebacker of the local college is arrested. Immediately media personalities go on air to plea for lenience from the judge. After all, "He's only a kid." But graduating high school makes you an adult. Or does it? This is just one of many examples that reveal how difficult it can be for teenagers to know if they are adults.

You can't expect your teenager to become an adult while confused about what that means. Such confusion leads to teenagers requiring more time to grow up.[2] The goal of this book is to equip you to launch your teenager into adulthood (and give you another ten years to use their vacant room as a study). But to do that you must know what makes an adult. And your teenager should too.

Many cultures have clear-cut lines to separate childhood and adulthood.[3] These lines are known as rites of passage. When the lines clearly are drawn, it becomes easy to know if you are an adult.

America has become a homogenization of many immigrating cultures. In doing so, it has lost many of the rites of passage various cultures brought here. Western culture mostly has abandoned the concept of rites of passage.[4]

Christians have joined the secular community in deserting the clear-cut lines that determined adulthood.[5] As a result, both Christian and secular teenagers wrestle with defining adulthood, and both delay becoming adults.[6]

You want your teenager to have a clear vision of adulthood and to know when adulthood arrives. Your family's rite of passage journey and ceremony will help accelerate this process.[7]

Here is exciting news for you. As a parent, the privilege of providing this powerful, equipping ceremony is given to you. You have the opportunity to move away from the ambiguous culture and do something valuable for your teenager.

The Bible and Rites of Passage

The Bible does not speak of rites of passage by name. There is not a "Thou shalt provide meaningful developmental milestones for thy children" verse.

Within the culture of the Bible, rites of passage happened naturally. A father would teach his son a profession until he was ready to set up shop on his own. Perhaps the son was sent to an apprentice. But the sending out or the setting up shop was the rite of passage. Everyone in the village would recognize the child's becoming an adult as a process. This was much clearer than in our culture today.

There may not be explicit rite of passage verses, but many teenagers in the Bible assumed adult responsibilities. Their community recognized their adultness. Josiah, Daniel, Esther, and Timothy demonstrate this. Their community recognized adultness in them before they were placed in leadership. Today, raising teenagers up in the way they should go ought to include following these biblical examples.[8]

What Makes a Rite of Passage Meaningful

Successful rites of passage provide clear markers for adulthood. After participation in the rite of passage journey, your teen will be able to say, "I know I am now an adult because an adult embodies the values taught to me by my family and mentors. By making these values my own, I declare my ascension to adulthood." In other words, a meaningful rite of passage celebrates the ownership of a well-defined set of values that give meaning to life.[9]

In addition, a rite of passage outlines a well-defined process of how to move into adulthood.[10] Typically this involves some sort of affirmation of values that identify the difference between childhood and adulthood. Your teenager should have a role in choosing those values and in shaping his or her own rite of passage.

Rites of passage strengthen and support values and truths by steering teenagers into the greater adult community. A team of mentoring adults gives teenagers a support system that says in unison, We value and affirm the direction of your life to the point that we say you are one of us.[11]

As the most influential person in your teenager's life, you need to take ownership of this journey into adulthood. A rite of passage is not something you pass off to your pastor or youth minister. As veteran youth expert Walker Moore states, "The burden of this rich and meaningful experience falls on the parents."[12] The idea of developing your own approach might seem scary. While it will take work and planning on your part, it does not need to fill you with anxiety.

If the idea of a rite of passage seems interesting to you, you might want to view it as one of seven celebrations and milestones in your offspring's life. These milestones, developed by Brian Haynes, are birth of a baby, faith commitment, preparing for adolescence, commitment to purity, passage to adulthood, high school graduation, and life in Christ. To see how your church and family can experience the milestones together, see *legacymilestones.com*.

Characteristics of Rites of Passage

Effective rites of passage contain three key phases:

1. the founding,

2. the instruction, and

3. the ceremony.

What makes the three-stage process work is the ownership of the process by your teenager. Ownership will lead your teenager to believe adulthood is possible at an age earlier than what culture suggests.[13]

Once this takes place, it is your responsibility as a parent to reinforce that ownership by seeing the teenager in a new light. Encourage key adults such as the pastor or student minister to do the same. Encourage leaders to ask your teen to be more involved or assume more adult behavior in your faith community.[14]

The founding phase. A rite of passage ceremony usually takes place during the teenage years. The founding phase and the instruction phase precede that ceremony and often take place during childhood.

The founding phase is your declaring to your child of your intentions to have a specific destination for him. This is your stating that you will intentionally nurture your child in a way that prepares her to be a mature follower of Christ. Essentially, you are communicating to your child that you will design a plan of parenting that has adulthood as the final destination.

These conversations could happen at any time. Starting early gives you advantages, but if you missed a few years, it is not the end of the world. The best time to plant a tree in your yard is ten years ago. The second best time is today.

Founding gives you a purpose and a direction for what comes next—the instruction phase. Begin now to have conversations with your child about new purposes you have in your parenting strategy. Help them see you are preparing them for adulthood.

The instruction phase. During the founding phase, you tell your child your goal is to parent him toward adulthood. During the instruction phase, you teach and prepare your child to be that adult. You must have a well-defined process of instruction that will help your child get to that goal.[15] Both founding and instruction take place before the actual rite of passage ceremony.

The instruction process will be covered in the next chapter in much greater detail. For now just understand that this is the most important part of the rite of passage process. As Tim Elmore suggests, "Adults must teach their kids to be value-driven people."[16]

Christian adults should ascribe to numerous values and virtues throughout Scripture. How do you emphasize them all? Ultimately the Holy Spirit must guide you to choose which values will receive the most emphasis as you guide your teenager to adulthood.

This may seem a daunting task. Tim Elmore and Walker Moore study the transitions from teenager to adult, and they have noted some key virtues that are lacking in emerging adults today. Their research may influence your instruction phase plans. Here is what they see a lack of:

- Integrity or honesty

- Selflessness and personal sacrifice

- Dependability

- A desire to leave a legacy

- Purity[17]

Plan to involve the greater adult faith community that surrounds your teenager during the instruction phase. As Kara Powell explains, "The more adults who seek out the student and help them apply faith to their daily life,

unless the virtues and values of adulthood are taught and then internalized by the teenager. Parents take the lead in this process.

The ceremony is important, but it only can affirm what already exists. With rites of passage, the journey to the ceremony carries much more weight than the ceremony itself. Much like baptism, the heart change must exist prior to the ceremony. If not, your teenager is just "getting wet." Ideally, you will teach values that lead to heart change.[23]

The Ceremony

When is the ideal time to have the ceremony? Most experts recommend between the ages of 13 and 15 to help accelerate your teen to adulthood.[24] If your teenager is older than that, here is some good news. Many meaningful rites of passage ceremonies have happened at ages 17, 18, or even 19. But whatever target date you choose, give yourself time to develop the adult virtues you want your teen to embrace.

It helps if the ceremony happens at a time of natural transition— from elementary school to middle school, middle school to high school, high school to college, or some other time of transition. The age of your teenager is not nearly as important as actually going through the process to help your son or daughter become an adult.

As you forge a rite of passage for your teenager, remember he or she needs to have a say in planning for the ceremony to be meaningful. First, the teenager needs to select the other adults who will participate in the service.[25] These are adults who are meaningful to your child, not necessarily to you. Don't be afraid to invite a non-Christian adult. Just think of the powerful witnessing tool this ceremony will be for the lost adult.

Second, after all the coaching and instruction from you, teenagers need to select what values and virtues are important to them.[26] Their code of conduct should reflect how they define adulthood, flowing out of all the instruction you have provided since birth.

Finally, talk openly with your teenager. Becoming an adult can be an anxious time. Take the time to explore your teen's emotions and discuss how he is feeling about the entire experience.

Remember to share the excitement of this time as well. Spider-Man had great responsibility, but he also got to swing from the rooftops. Adults do get to experience and interact with the world in different and sometimes more fun and engaging ways than children.

Three Examples of Rite of Passage Ceremonies

To help give you a clear picture of what a rite of passage ceremony might look like, here are three ceremonies actual families have experienced.

Example 1. You and your teenager meet together to select five adults (same sex as your teenager) both of you admire. Once this list is complete, your teenager can ask all of these adults to spend one day together. They could do anything during the day, such as fishing, shopping, or serving at a homeless shelter. But at some point during the day, each selected adult is to share one spiritual truth and one piece of life advice with your teenager.

Once all five adults have spent a day with your teenager, select a time to gather everyone together for a celebratory meal. At the dinner plan for your teenager, share truths that he has learned and how he is applying those truths. End the night with everyone affirming and praying for your child who is now an adult.[27]

Example 2. You and your teenager work together to select five to seven virtues (honor, faithfulness, compassion, etc.) she thinks represent a godly woman. Then consider adults who have a positive influence on your teenager. Assign an adult to be responsible for each virtue. Ask them to prepare a spoken challenge for your teenager and provide a gift for her that symbolizes the assigned adult virtue. For example, the virtue "honor" might be represented by someone who served in the military. The gift could be a uniform patch or a replica medal.

Gather everyone together for a special night of challenges and gifts for your teenager. Once everyone has finished, invite your teenager to summarize the instruction and gifts received. Conclude the evening by having the adults affirm these virtues and praying over your teenager.

Example 3. Give your teenager the assignment to develop a personal code of conduct. ("An adult is responsible." "An adult is full of integrity." Etc.) Once finished, work with your teenager to select influential mentors. Ask each mentor to take one aspect of the code of conduct and instruct your teenager on how to live up to that virtue.

Arrange for a special day of instruction. Drive your teenager to the first mentor who will share a lesson. Then the first mentor will drive your teenager to the second mentor, who will carry on in like fashion until the last mentor drives your teen to a restaurant or other gathering place. The day ends with a meal and ceremony where your teenager publicly and prayerfully adopts the code of conduct.

Conclusion

You likely have read this chapter with your own teenager in mind. That is as it should be. But be open to the possibility that the Spirit might prompt you to seek out one or two teenagers in your faith community who do not have godly parents. By His leading, you may choose to pull those teenagers into your family and include them in a rites of passage journey.

Sadly, few families inside or outside the church provide rites of passage ceremonies. This probably will be uncharted territory for you. You may feel uncomfortable or a little nervous.

Just remember that rites of passage are powerful tools that can accelerate your teenager toward adulthood. Anything of value requires effort. So be prepared to spend days and weeks in prayer as you choose values that seem most important. Then plan how to celebrate those values as you create lasting memories for your teenager.

Lean on your team of adult mentors for ideas as well. James says there is wisdom in the counsel of many. Together you can tailor the instruction process and rite of passage ceremony that will be just right for your teenager.

People are unique, and your family's ceremony might look very different from another family's. In fact, if you have multiple children, their ceremonies might not resemble one another's. That is completely fine as long as you keep the vision clear.

Most importantly, find strength and vision from the Holy Spirit for your entire rite of passage journey. He will give you the inspiration to prepare a meaningful milestone on the road to adulthood for your teenager.

CHAPTER 5: TEACHING YOUR TEENAGER WHAT ADULTS KNOW

Doug Bischoff

Your intentional conversations can teach your teenagers what they need to know to be adults.

Thirty Minutes Matter

In 1986, executives at Domino's Pizza set out to make a bold guarantee. They promised that if they could not deliver your pizza in "30 minutes or less" you would get a free pizza.[1] People all over America began counting down the minutes to see if Domino's would truly deliver.

Near the end of that same decade, NBC began a new show called *Seinfeld*. By the last episode the show commanded the attention of almost 80 million viewers.[2] In just 30 minutes, Seinfeld was able to impact the language, the customs, and the sense of humor of many people around the world, not to mention making an incredible impact on sitcoms.

30 Minutes Together at Home

Parents have the potential to move their teenagers toward adulthood as they invest just 30 minutes at a time to help them understand truths, both spiritual and practical. These truths can lead teenagers to someday walk with God on their own as mature and healthy adults.

Imagine a couple nights each week set aside to pass along the things known by a parent and needed by a teenager. Short, 30-minute conversations could move a parent from wishing, hoping, and dreaming of someday putting a plan together to actually living out a regular time to disciple and prepare their children.

These skills would benefit teenagers and move them toward adulthood. However, our current culture often lacks the delivery system to provide these skills to teenagers. As described in a previous chapter, teenagers of past generations spent much more time with family, especially parents, to learn the skills needed in life.

As a parent you may not be aware of all the skills you have acquired to this point in your life. If you were to sit down and make a list of everything you know how to do, especially those skills learned as an adult, it could be quite a list. Consider skills such as cooking, balancing a checking account, paying bills, writing a check, cleaning the house, putting gas in the car, landscaping a yard, buying a car, interviewing for a job, creating a resume, changing an HVAC filter, doing laundry, studying the Bible, sharing Christ with a friend, choosing quality friendships, deciding which candidate will get your vote, keeping a calendar, or discerning God's will.

Besides specific life skills, you need a way to transfer your values and virtues to the heart of your teenager. As described in the previous chapter, a rite of passage is the celebration of the journey in which teenagers receive these values and virtues from you. Ahead of that ceremony, you need many focused conversations to ensure your values and virtues are understood and embraced.

To prepare your teenager for a healthy adulthood in which skills and beliefs are owned, you prayerfully can begin a systematic and intentional approach. You likely will create planned times set aside to deliver these skills and values to your children. Just as a baseball or soccer team decides on a schedule for games and practices, families also can agree on times each week they will meet to practice the launch into adulthood.

Consider these possible results:

- if you have 30-minute, focused conversations three nights a week,

- if you do this just 40 of the 52 weeks of the year,

- if you do this the six years you have a teenager at home,

- that would be 720 focused conversations by high school graduation.

What could your teenager learn, embrace, and come to value through that many well-planned conversations? How would your teenager's preparation for adulthood compare with most teenagers today?

These conversations bring intentionality and purpose to the desire many parents possess—to give their children a foundation of life lessons to propel them into adulthood. On some nights the family could forgo the sitcom and sit down together for active learning, maybe while they wait for a pizza to be delivered.

Format of 30-Minute Sessions

Movement! If you've ever had the difficult task of moving something large such as a couch or a desk, you understand the importance of movement. Often it feels as if the weight of the object is just too much for you to get to your destination. Then comes movement. It doesn't have to be a great amount, but it does indicate that you are not where you were.

Teaching and preparing a teenager for adulthood often can feel weighty. What a parent needs is some type of movement toward the goal. Planning and leading 30-minute conversations can be that first movement.

Your son might ask, "Dad, how do you decide when it's time to change the oil in the car?" Or your daughter might ask, "How can we know what God is telling us to do in a given situation?"

Think about sitting around the dinner table or in the family room of your home, talking as a family about what your kids need to know. Teenagers are engaged because they desire to know more about the adult world. Parents are engaged as they are excited to share what they know with their kids. Families are strengthened as they interact, spend time together, and grow through an intentional plan of moving your teenager toward being an adult.

So, what does intentionally creating movement look like? Imagine having the following schedule for your family as a way of passing on skills and knowledge:

- Monday evening—Basic discipleship focused on who Christ is and who you are in Christ.

- Tuesday and Thursday evenings—Basic life skills, everything from choosing a mate to changing the oil in the car.

- Wednesday nights could be free for church activities, and all other nights are left available for sports, clubs, hobbies, and other family activities. Of course, nights other than Monday, Tuesday, and Thursday might work better in the rhythm of your family.

These conversations are not designed to take up an entire evening, only 30 minutes. This time could be spent over the dinner table after a family meal or in the driveway as mom or dad teaches a practical skill.

In the appendix you will find a list of more than one hundred topics you might cover. Imagine how much your kids could pick up in covering each topic several times. The appendix also will direct you to a website teaching modules created by other parents, youth ministers, and other concerned adults.

For this plan to succeed, a regular meeting place is a great place to start. Ask your teenager what spot seems best for talking and listening. Or consider where your family already spends time talking the most freely and make that your meeting place each Monday, Tuesday, and Thursday. Be sure to avoid distractions from media. Make those 30 minutes a no-interrupt time where dad doesn't answer his phone or check e-mail and teenagers don't attempt to listen to music or play games. Commit to focus for just 30 minutes on an important topic.

Also consider a time of evening that keeps everyone engaged. Dad or mom may need some time to regroup after work, or kids may have homework that needs to be completed so they can focus. Choose a time that best fits the schedule for both generations and commit to it.

Preparing to Lead

Mom or dad should take the lead in preparing the 30-minute teaching conversations or in downloading prepared modules online. Remember to leave time for discussion. This is not the time for parents to do their best impersonation of a college lecturer. Teenagers need the freedom to ask questions and to talk through things they don't understand. The prepared modules are broken into the four following categories of learners:

- Novice—For teenagers just getting started in learning spiritual or practical truths.

- Apprentice—More scriptural references and ideas to go deeper into truth.

- Master—Helps teenagers own their faith by asking tough questions. Prepares them to explain or defend their faith.

- Master/Teacher—Opportunity for teenagers to teach the module at the Novice or Apprentice level to younger siblings or peers, with parents still in the room to provide feedback.

The goal is teenagers who know the truth, understand the truth, embrace the truth, teach the truth, and defend the truth. The ultimate goal is teenagers who have assumed responsibility for their faith walk.

If you decide to write your own content, you may benefit from looking over the online modules as a template. Include the following elements in each session and think through where in the process of learning your teenager is currently (novice, apprentice, master, master/ teacher):

- Why are we looking at this or why is this important?

- How do you do this, or what do you need to learn?

- What questions do you have, or what doesn't make sense?

- How does this relate to who Christ is or who I am in Christ?

Kingdom impact must be the lens through which each module is presented. In other words, why does this matter in my relationship with Christ? Or how does my knowing this bring glory to God? In regards to topics such as interpreting Scripture or sharing Christ, the implications are fairly obvious. But you also can show how topics such as maintaining a car or a house require a spiritual application or connection to stewardship.

Keeping It Fresh

Investing in your teenager can feel a lot like exercise. You want to do it, you know you need to do it, but doing it well and consistently takes discipline. Here are a few ideas to help you get over the obstacles that might get in your way. (These also work on exercise, by the way).

God. Sound impossible? It's not! Every discovery you make can soon deepen the spiritual walk of your teenager. And teenagers may learn even more just from watching your struggle to grow.

For many adults spiritual growth consists of "more of the same"— more sermons, more songs, more Bible reading, or more retreats or conferences. But what is the result of all this "more"? Typically the result is little actual growth. Perhaps the reason is that sermons, songs, Bible reading, and retreats are meant to spark growth within the context of a relationship with the one true God. It's not that adults don't have that relationship; they just don't attempt to grow first in the relationship before adding spiritual activity.

Scripture demonstrates that spiritual truths are best shared through relationships. Elisha had Elijah, Timothy had Paul, and the disciples had Jesus. It wasn't just the words these spiritual mentors shared that impacted the lives of these people. It was the daily living and the relationship that filled in all the gaps. Any discipleship you do with your teenager must be mirrored in a daily relationship of love and warmth with them.

This is not to say you don't provide reasonable and firm discipline. It just means that the relationship is not sacrificed for a moment of indulgence in anger. Recently my son said to me, "Dad, none of my friends have talks with their dads. Why is that?" I didn't really have an answer. I love the opportunity to talk with my son about baseball, school, growing up, or whatever else is on his mind. And he enjoys it, too!

Practical Matters

Begin your focused conversations by asking your kids the high point and low point of their day. Get them talking by asking questions you know they will answer. By creating conversation, you begin the process of engaging them for discipleship. Avoid the use of lecture. It usually leads to that "glossed over" look from your teenagers. Include them in the process by asking questions along the way that give them the opportunity to stay plugged in to what you are saying.

Teenagers often learn by talking through truths they don't yet understand. You can aid this by avoiding yes and no questions. Rather than asking, "Is forgiveness good?" try saying, "Tell me a time when you felt forgiven by someone and why it was important to you." This gives teenagers the chance to work through their understanding of the subject.

Don't feel as though you must teach everything about a given subject. Remember you have six years to continue to develop the message. This also gives you time to learn more about the subject and grow in your understanding of it.

Look for resources that will allow you to learn more, such as Christian websites. Your church library also may have many resources available to prepare you to lead out in discipleship. Ask church leaders or other parents to suggest materials they have used and found helpful. Take advantage of conferences offered by your church or other churches in your area. Look for past sermons by your pastor your family can listen to and then discuss. Or use the past week's sermon as your topic each week to facilitate discussion.

Spiritual Orphans

No one likes being left out. From the time we are children and experience our first time of being picked last or seeing a group of friends "forget" to include us, we know how it feels for others to have something we don't. In your church or in the circle of friends your teenager keeps, some kids likely don't have anyone discipling or pouring into them.

There are several reasons for spiritual orphans. Their parents may not know the Lord, or perhaps they have been hurt by a church experience and have removed themselves from a biblical community. Whatever the reason, these teenagers should be on our radar. They need and require the same mentoring and preparation as your own teenager.

Consider for a moment how easy it would be to invite another teenager, who doesn't have a spiritual mentor, to join you and your family. No additional study modules would be necessary, and it really wouldn't require anything other than an invitation and possibly a little bit of logistical work. Now consider the impact this invitation could have on that teenager.

The Search Institute, an organization devoted to "discovering what kids need to succeed," has created a list of 40 developmental assets needed in the lives of teenagers, age 12–18.[3] The list is based on years of research. Among the 40 assets are the need for other adult relationships and for caring neighborhoods. Both of these assets could be achieved through the inclusion of a teenager without a spiritual influence in his life.

Consider a friend of your teenager at church or in your neighborhood that could benefit from being included in your family times of teaching and discipleship. Think about ways you could invite them or introduce them to this kind of discipleship. Maybe you could begin by just sharing with them who Christ is to you. You might be surprised how interested your teenager would be in having a friend be part of your time together as a family.

If, however, your teenager shows resentment or jealousy, take advantage of the opportunity to speak with him about the needs of others. If it's distracting or hinders your teen's growth, wait until she is ready for a friend to join.

But be conscious of the myriad of teenagers without someone to lead them toward adulthood. Also consider the consequences experienced by our culture each day from young adults that never really found their way into mature adulthood.

Walking Their Own Path

Jimmy was really embarrassed. It was the first day of fifth grade, and he had walked around all day with his shoe untied. Several people had pointed out that he needed to tie his shoe, but it remained unlaced. Finally a teacher asked Jimmy if he could please tie his shoe. Then came the embarrassment as Jimmy revealed he could not. He had never learned this basic life lesson. He needed someone to do it for him.

At some point your teenager must take responsibility for his own spiritual walk. If your teenager decides to have a rich, vibrant, and fresh walk with God, then he must make investments in his own spiritual life. Your son or daughter needs to know how to study the Bible, to pray, to share Christ with others, and to discern the will of God.

Consider giving your older teenager the opportunity to choose the discussion topics for a month from the list in the appendix. Encourage her to take a night to lead the family instead of mom or dad. Use the master/teacher section of the online modules to facilitate this teaching. Show her how you prepare and what you do to make sure you have something to offer the rest of the family.

Another great opportunity for older teens is to have them meet monthly with younger kids in the family to talk with them about what they are learning. One of the best ways to learn more deeply is to explain what you have learned so that others can understand it. Encourage teenagers to become lifelong learners and lifelong disciplers.

Walking with God

You desire for your teenager to walk with God. Walking with God involves learning new things and applying what you have learned. One of the best ways to encourage your teen in this is to ask, "What are you learning right now from God's Word?"

This question implies some important things. First, it points out the importance of a relationship with God that is growing, not stagnant. Nobody likes to stay in the same place. If you have a hobby, you want to get better at it. If you have a skill, you want to improve. If you are at level one, you want to get to level two. Growth is part of life.

By encouraging your kids to be learning from God's Word, you teach them to expect to learn something from God's Word. Have you ever read the Bible without an intentional desire to learn? Was the reading beneficial to your life? Probably not! By reading and applying God's Word, you grow.

Second, the question points out the importance of God's Word being a part of their faith walk. If you've ever been to a Vacation Bible School, you know and have heard often the importance of the B-I-B- L-E. God's Word is the textbook of life. Encourage your kids to read it, to learn form it, and then to apply it.

Teenagers can struggle with applying God's Word, believing that because the writings are so old, they have no relevance to today's culture. However, the lust, greed, jealousy, forgiveness, repentance, and love found in the Bible are just as much a part of our lives today. Make sure your kids love God's Word and ask for that love in prayer.

Conclusion

An investment can be made in many different ways. It can be an investment of time, money, wisdom, or skill. But the point of any investment is the same—a good return. What is the return you hope to see in the life of your son or daughter? What do you hope they know and understand as they walk across that college campus for the first time?

The investment of just 30 minutes a few times a week could radically impact the answer to those questions. American entrepreneur, writer, and investor Robert Arnott said, "In investing, what is comfortable is rarely profitable."[4] The change needed to allow your teenager to own a personal faith and walk with Christ in a difficult culture may not be comfortable. It may require changes in schedule, priorities, and family rhythm. But the return on this investment likely will far exceed any monetary investment a parent ever makes.

CHAPTER 6: PREPARING YOUR TEENAGER TO WORK AND EARN A LIVING

David Odom

You can give your teenager a strong work ethic and a focused way to move toward a vocation.

In order to prepare your teenager to work and earn a living, your teenager needs practical experiences in various work environments. You can provide your children with resources and experiences designed to help them discover the right career. If you don't want to wake up one day with an unemployed 25-year-old living in your basement, then you can take decisive steps to help your teenager effectively move into the workforce.

The Problem

Today's employers report that young adults lack basic skills in communication, creativity, and teamwork.[1] They seem lazy and lack a strong work ethic. More and more the teenagers entering young adulthood are not prepared for the real world.[2] Research indicates that career indecision at age 16 can negatively affect financial earnings at age 26.[3] When young people make early career decisions, they are better prepared for adulthood.[4] This chapter will help you prepare your teenager to confidently enter the workforce and earn a living.

The Importance and Value of Work

The average American works just under nine hours a day.[5] This adds up to an average workweek of 45 hours. That's 2,340 hours per year and 105,300 hours over a lifetime. In addition, the amount of time a person spends at work on a given day outweighs time spent on anything else. The average American sleeps 32 percent of the day (7.6 hours). Thirty- seven percent of the day is spent in work-related activity, leaving 31 percent of the day for family, leisure, and other activities.

Why these stats? Because of how much time you spend at work, your job has a tremendous influence on how you live your life. Your job affects where you live and who your friends are. Doesn't it make sense that God would be concerned with something that consumes most of your time?

God Is a Worker

The first step in preparing your teenager to earn a living is demonstrating the importance of work. The Bible teaches that work has intrinsic value. The word *intrinsic* means "valuable by its essential nature."[6] One way we know work has intrinsic value is because the Bible describes God as a worker.[7] Consider Genesis 2:1–2: "Thus the heavens and the earth were completed, and all their hosts. By the seventh day God completed His *work* which He had done, and He rested on the seventh day from all His *work* which He had done" (emphasis added).

The work described in these verses refers to God's creative activity. God's creative work can also be seen in Psalm 8:3–4: "When I consider Your heavens, the *work* of Your fingers, the moon and the stars, which You have ordained; what is man that You take thought of him, and the son of man that You care for him?" (emphasis added).

Not only does the Bible describe God's past work, but it tells us God is still working: "But He answered them, 'My Father is *working* until now, and I Myself am *working*'" (John 5:17, emphasis added). In fact, God is at work today. The Bible tells us that God "upholds creation," meets needs, and works out His purposes and will (Heb. 1:3; Phil. 4:19; Eph. 1:11).

Work Is a Gift from God

Not only is God a worker, but the Bible also tells us God created people to be workers.[8] Genesis 1:28–29 says: "God blessed them; and God said to them, 'Be fruitful and multiply, and fill the earth, and subdue it; and rule over the fish of the sea and over the birds of the sky and over every living thing that moves on the earth.' Then God said, 'Behold, I have given you every plant yielding seed that is on the surface of all the earth, and every tree which has fruit yielding seed; it shall be food for you.'"

Look at the work described in Genesis 1:

- Govern the earth.

- Reign over the earth.

- Work the land.

Work clearly was part of God's design for humanity from the beginning. Work is a gift from God. Ecclesiastes 3:13 says: "And people should eat and drink and enjoy the fruits of their labor, for these are *gifts from God* " (NLT, emphasis added).

As a parent you play a vital role in your teenager's view of work.[9] You will be wise to help your teenager understand the intrinsic value of work. Talk to your teenager about the work of God and what a tremendous gift it is to be able to work. Share with your future adult the positive aspects of your own personal work experience.

Calling Versus Career

You may use the terms *vocation, career,* and *job* interchangeably, but they are not the same. The term *vocation* refers to one's "calling." The word has a Latin origin which means to "call after someone."[10] The term refers to work you are designed or fitted to do.[11] This is what gives your life meaning and purpose. It is overarching and doesn't necessarily refer to one specific job. It is the theme of your life.[12]

Career refers to a "line of work."[13] This is what fulfills your calling. It is broader than just the job you have now. It is a field or category of jobs. A job is a specific expression of your calling. You might have several jobs throughout your life that all are expression of your vocation.

Look at the Old Testament example of David:

- Calling or Vocation—"A man after [God's] own heart" (1 Sam. 13:14).

- Career—He was devoted to God through public service.

- Jobs—He was a shepherd, singer (in the king's court), soldier, and king.

What about you? Do you have a calling? Are you helping your future adult discover the calling and design of God? Look at the challenge found in Ephesians 5:15–17: "So be careful how you live. Don't live like fools, but like those who are *wise*. Make the most of every opportunity in these evil days. Don't act thoughtlessly, but *understand what the Lord wants you to do*" (NLT, emphasis added).

Be, Go, Do

Wise parents help teenagers discover what the Lord wants them to do. This process starts through prayer. You can teach your teenager to seek the Lord's will by remembering three little words: *be, go, do*. These three words form the basis of a simple prayer that expresses a humble and submissive heart:

> Lord, I'll be what You want me to be. I'll go where
> You want me to go. I'll do what You want me to do.

When your teenager prays this prayer and sincerely means it, a change in attitude can begin to take place. Instead of focusing on a career that offers the most money, a teenager can seek after the heart of God. Rather than emphasizing personal success or material gain, he or she submits to the will of God. When your teenager prays this prayer, he echoes the cry of Isaiah, "Here am I. Send me" (Isa. 6:8).

You can lead your teenager first by modeling this prayer. Say to God, "Lord, I'll be what You want me to be. I'll go where You want me to go. I'll do what You want me to do." And then pray something similar to this for your teenager: "Lord, help my teenager know what You want him to be. Show my teenager where You want her to go. And Lord, reveal to my teenager what You want him to do."

Before reading the next section, stop right now and pray for your teenager.

Developing a Strong Work Ethic

A strong work ethic is rare among today's young people. The number one complaint about teenagers in the workplace today is that they have a negative attitude toward work.[14]

Employers feel young people:

- Act entitled.

- Are impatient and unrealistic.

- Are lazy.

- Don't want to work hard to build a career.

- Want constant feedback and instant gratification.

- Don't show respect for others' experience. [15]

Adults must share some of the blame. According to an AP-Viacom survey, today's young people feel their school did not do an adequate job preparing them for work or helping them choose a career. [16] You can prepare your children for a future career by helping them understand the importance of a strong personal work ethic.

A strong work ethic includes a belief in the moral or intrinsic value of work. [17] As discussed in the first section, work has intrinsic value because God is a worker and work is His gift. As a Christian, your personal work ethic stems from a belief that you are working for God or on His behalf. Regardless of the type of work (custodian or doctor), you work for the Lord.

To have a strong work ethic also means that you are dependable. This means you do what you say you will do. If you say you will arrive at 8:00 AM, then you arrive at 8:00 AM—not 8:15 or 8:20 but at 8:00 AM. Employers value teenagers who are dependable.

Another component of a strong work ethic is honesty. This means doing what is right even when acting alone. It's easy to do the right thing if everyone else is going along. It's more difficult when you are the only one choosing to do what is right.

Honesty is a character trait that employers value. Teach your teenager that if he makes a mistake, he should admit it. If she breaks something, she shouldn't try to cover it up. Are you raising an honest teenager? Can your teenager be counted on to tell the truth in every situation? You can help your teenager develop honesty by rewarding it when you see it.

Young workers often complain about menial task they believe are beneath them. [18] However, the ability to work hard even when the task seems trivial is another important aspect of a strong work ethic. Teenagers need to understand how each job is vital to the overall operation of an organization. Each employee has an important role to play. Many seemingly menial tasks are the heart and soul of a company. Teenagers build trust with employers by working hard, no matter the circumstance.

Teenagers and a Strong Work Ethic

Many teenagers are not given opportunities to develop into dependable, honest, and hardworking employees. Teenagers need training in work- like environments. They need opportunities that will help develop these essential qualities. You can help your teenager develop a strong work ethic by providing positive work experiences.

Early work experiences can help your children:

- Build character.

- Learn to be on time to work.

- Finish what they start.

For instance, you can give your teenager responsibility to accomplish important tasks at home. You can challenge your son or daughter to learn new skills to benefit themselves and others. Ask yourself: What does my teenager need to learn? How to clean the fireplace? How to change a tire? How to pay bills? Why doesn't she know how to do that yet? How can I best teach my child?[19] You can provide growth- producing feedback for both teenage successes and failures.[20]

Encourage your teenager not to give up and quit a job when work is hard. Explain the important role each person has in an organization. Help your young people understand that work is important even when it seems menial and mundane. The end of this chapter will provide specific examples of work experiences that can be useful to teenagers.

How Teenagers Can Find a Job to Love

Examine God's Design

God has uniquely designed your teenager. No one else has the exact same skills, talents, abilities, experiences, and personality. This is part of God's design.

For example, look at how God designed David: "But David said to Saul, 'Your servant was tending his father's sheep. When a lion or a bear came and took a lamb from the flock, I went out after him and attacked him, and rescued it from his mouth; and when he rose up against me, I seized him by his beard and struck him and killed him. Your servant has killed both the lion and the bear; and this uncircumcised Philistine will be like one of them, since he has taunted the armies of the living God.' And David said, 'The Lord who delivered me from the paw of the lion and from the paw of the bear, He will deliver me from the hand of this Philistine.' And Saul said to David, 'Go, and may the Lord be with you'" (1 Sam. 17:34–37).

What types of skills and abilities does it take to kill a lion or a bear? Certainly it would take:

- Courage
- Strength
- Skill or technique
- Endurance

Of course, the spirit of God was with David to help him accomplish these amazing tasks, but God's design for David was also at work. He was born with some of these qualities and abilities, and others he developed over time. But the Bible is clear that God made David for a purpose. And God has a purpose for your teenager!

You can help your teenager find purpose in life by examining God's design. God has designed each person with unique physical and mental abilities as well as different likes and dislikes. You can help your teenager discover God's design by asking probing questions such as:

- Are you an outdoor or an indoor person?

- Are you a thinker or a feeler?

- Are your strengths more athletic or academic?

- Do you pay attention to detail or like to see the big picture?

You can help your young people find a match between the way God made him and jobs that require compatible skills, abilities, and personality.[21] A number of resources are available to help your teenager discover God's design. Here's a review of three popular resources:

Clifton StrengthsFinder.™ See *www.strengthsquest.com.* StrengthsQuest is part of the Gallup research group. The Clifton StrengthsFinder assessment is an online tool designed to help high school and college students discover natural strengths—the way they naturally feel, think, or behave. The assessment takes about 30 minutes to complete. Afterward, your student receives a customized report that lists his or her top five "talent themes." The report also includes "action items" designed to help your teenager develop those strengths.

Finally, the report includes suggestions on how your young person might use the talents to achieve academic, career, and personal success. The StrengthsQuest book provides an overview of the strengths and 34 themes.[22] You get a free access code for the assessment with the purchase of the book. If you just want your student to take the assessment, it will cost less, but you also receive access to the online version of the StrengthsQuest book.

MAPP™ (*assessment.com*). MAPP stands for Motivational Appraisal of Personal Potential. The test consists of 71 questions with three answers. Your teenager picks the statement he or she likes the most and the one he or she likes the least. After your teenager completes the assessment, the test provides a list of career categories and jobs based on the responses. The initial assessment is free, but to access all the results requires payment. The Starter Package gives your student access to 50 possible careers linked to the Department of Labor's O*Net jobs database.

The package includes access to the complete Occupational Outlook Handbook that gives details for each job on the personalized report. Your teenager will be able to view job requirements, what an average day on the job is like, pay range, and training or educational requirements. Other packages cost more but provide more job listings and additional resources. Although the cost associated with viewing results is high, your teenager will receive a tremendous amount of information that can lead to a deeper understanding of God's design.

Myers-Briggs Type Indicator® (MBTI®). This is the most well-known and effective personality test. It was developed by Isabel Briggs Myers and her mother, Katharine Briggs. The assessment is based on the work of psychologist Carl G. Jung to identify personality types.[23] The MBTI provides a series of multiple-choice questions with no right or wrong answers. Your teenager simply indicates a preference. Following the assessment, your teenager will be identified with one of the 16 personality types. A detailed description of the personality type and possible career choices is also provided.

Identifying personality type can be useful in career planning because your teenager can discover which careers and jobs he or she might be more comfortable pursuing. For instance, a young adult with an introverted personality type may be more comfortable doing individual research, while an extrovert may prefer more interaction with people. The official tests are usually administered by professionals who are trained to explain test results and apply them to suitable careers.

However, the makers of the MBTI also provide an online option (mbticomplete.com) that does not require professional interpretation. It provides a comprehensive description of your personality type and an explanation of compatible careers. It is well worth the financial investment. If your teenager just wants to know what his or her personality type is, many free versions of the MBTI are available online. Yet most eventually require a fee to view results that match with jobs or careers.

Job Exploration Sheet

In addition to these formal assessments, you can begin to help your teenager discover God's design by simply asking a series of leading questions. Ask your teenager to complete the Job Exploration Sheet below. Responses will begin to give your teenager an idea of God's design and what types of jobs might be a good fit.

Who I Am

- What are your strengths and weaknesses?

- In what situations do you feel at your best?

- What are you passionate about?

Occupations to Explore

- What are your top five career choices?

- What do these career choices require?

- What type of education is needed?

- What school subjects must be mastered?

- Do these occupations match who you are?

Discuss responses and challenge your young person to explore one or two of the occupations in detail. Suggest reading a biography about someone in a chosen career, writing a letter to someone in that line of work, or conducting interviews of people in specific jobs. Encourage teenagers to investigate specific training requirements, the best schools, working conditions, and the necessary personal attributes.[24]

A Job Your Teenager Does Not Love

In addition to discussing how to find a job your teenager will love, talk about the reality of working in a career she doesn't love. For instance, when the perfect job is not available, what should your future adult do? Not work? Sit around the house playing video games? No, as discussed above, all work is a gift from God. There is value in work, even in a job you don't love.

Working in a job you don't love can:

- Provide for you and your family.

- Build character and work experience useful in the future.

- Meet needs and provide important services.

As you discuss finding a job your teenager can love, review with your teenager why all work has value. Appreciating the value of work itself is the key. This is why it is important to build appreciation for work while your teenager is young and still living at home. To this end, the final section of the chapter discusses the value of job practice through serving, volunteering, and part-time work.

Practicing and Preparing for a Future Job

During the transition from high school to full-time work, teenagers are preparing for adult careers.[25] To successfully transition to adulthood, teenagers should be exposed to a wide range of experiences such as community service, volunteering, and part-time work.

Reclaim Saturday for Work

Many young adults are shocked by the transition from the jobless, carefree days of high school and college to the realities of work and career. Youth need experience in work environments to help ease this transition. For most students Saturday offers the best opportunity to build work experience. Positioned between school days and church, Saturday is the ideal day for job training.

But you may ask, "How can I make my teenager give up Saturday?" Saturday has become a day for young people to sleep in late, hang out with friends, and rest from a busy week. Admittedly, it won't be easy at first. But ask yourself, "By getting my teenager up and doing something purposeful on Saturday, am I hurting or helping in the long run?" The answer, of course, is that you are helping your teenager.

Here are a few suggestions to help you reclaim Saturday for work:

- Don't immediately claim every Saturday for work. Start small, maybe once a month, and then gradually build up to using every Saturday for work preparation.

- Set a date and time. Post your job practice experiences on the family calendar. Guard the time and don't allow other activities to override job practice.

- Avoid the urge to link job practice with financial gain. Don't bribe your teenager by offering money as an incentive. The real reward will be work experience.

- Focus on relationships. Relationships are important to today's teenagers.[26] Family and friends can be significant motivators for job preparation. You can leverage the relationships in your teenager's life to create motivation to get job practice. Whether working around the house as a family or serving the community with friends, teenagers work best in the context of relationships.

Serving

One way to gain work experience is through community service. Invite your teenager to choose a local community service project. It might be helping at a soup kitchen, delivering Meals on Wheels, or picking up trash. Involve your entire family. Find a need in your area that can be met by your family working together. Then invite your teenager's close friends to participate.

Service opportunities include:

- Church mission projects
- Nursing home visits
- Community clean-up events
- Stocking shelves at local food bank
- Raking leaves for a senior adult

Volunteering

The next phase of job practice involves volunteering on a regular basis. Serving and volunteering can seem synonymous. The difference between the two as it relates to job practice is that volunteering is usually more frequent and focused.

Use the Job Exploration Sheet to choose a job or career of interest for your teenager. Then seek ways to volunteer in that field of work. Many employers would welcome the help from a teenage volunteer. In fact, in many states, volunteering is the only legal option for those under age 15 or 16. And don't forget, as your teenager gains work experience on the job, volunteering can lead to opportunities for part-time work.

Here are a few ways to help your young person find a volunteer job:

- Arrange an interview with a local business owner to ask questions about the job or career.

- Bring your teenager with you to work and let him shadow you throughout your day.

- Ask church members about volunteer opportunities.

To add value to volunteering, invite your teenager to discuss those experiences. This debriefing time is essential to help your teenager make connections with future career options. Invite her to discuss observations about the job or working conditions.[27] Ask:

- What did you learn today?

- What was hard about the job?

- What did you like about the job?

- Can you see yourself doing this type of job as a career?

Working Part-time

The next step in job practice is part-time employment. When your teenager is ready for the responsibility of steady employment, a part- time job can provide valuable work experience. Many industries rely heavily on teenage part-time employees. Examples of part-time work can include fast-food restaurants, retail stores, and clerical work. You can help your young person select a job that has the potential to be a positive experience.

Conclusion

You may be overwhelmed by the material covered in this chapter. Don't let it immobilize you. Be proactive! Start today! Begin small. Talk about career interest with your teenager and find ways to serve as a family. With your support and guidance, these preparations will help your teenager find a job and earn a living.

CHAPTER 7: PREPARATION FOR MARRIAGE AND FAMILY

David Booth

Your high school graduate can be ready for marriage and family whenever God should so lead.

A Titanic Tragedy

As a younger youth minister, one of the annual youth ministry duties I dreaded was Graduation Sunday. Among the celebratory pomp and circumstance of high school seniors dressed in cap and gown was a gnawing ache that something was about to go terribly wrong for many of them.

Like the celebrated *RMS Titanic* beginning its historic maiden (and only) voyage across the Atlantic, I couldn't help but feel that graduates were similarly ill prepared for the largely hidden icebergs that threatened beneath the surface. On April 15, 1912, what was formerly thought of as an unsinkable ship became a casket under the sea for 1,512 (68 percent) of the 2,224 trusting crew members and passengers.

Today's church teenager naively faces the perilous seas of emerging adulthood, unlikely to survive unscathed:

- 95% of emerging adults will have sexual intercourse before marriage, 84% before age 24, and 64% with a partner other than their eventual spouse.[1]

- 64% of 18–45-year-old husbands and 60% of wives report having cohabited (lived together) before marriage; 22% of husbands and 18% of wives have done so more than once before marriage.[2]

These numbers represent an unprecedented shift in values and practices deviously touted by American culture as advancement in the pursuit of individual and marriage happiness. Sending 18-year-olds unprepared into these treacherous seas increases the likelihood they themselves will succumb to these powerful, destructive life perspectives and relationship strategies.

Cohabitation, for example, remains one the most popular proposed remedies to failing marriages.

However, those who cohabit experience:

- Less closeness, stability, and happiness.

- Twice as many fights and five times more violence.

- Five times higher relationship failure before marriage and 50–80 percent higher divorce rates after marriage.

- Less faithfulness. Men are four times less faithful, and women are eight times less faithful to their eventual marriage partner.[3]

"Not far beneath the surface appearance of happy, liberated emerging adult sexual adventure and pleasure lies a world of hurt, insecurity, confusion, inequality, shame, and regret."[4] Why are Christian emerging adults so vulnerable to destructive patterns of the world?

Emerging Adults Are Vulnerable

Cultural and developmental characteristics make emerging adults susceptible to damaging perspectives on life. Researchers have noted inflated individualism in unprepared emerging adults.[5] Individualism amplifies cohabitation, prolonged singleness, and marriage alternatives marked by a lack of commitment and adult responsibility.[6]

Developmental psychologist Erik Erikson pointed to the fact that as people move from childhood to adulthood, there is an innate, relentless drive for identity followed by intimacy.[7] For today's teenagers and emerging adults, however, development has been reordered with dire consequences. Intimacy has become the pervasive *method* for discovering personal identity rather than the *by-product* of identity.

Emerging Adults Do Not Want to Betray Self

Thinking as an unprepared emerging adult will help you understand the kind of preparation necessary to accelerate adult-like maturity in your sons and daughters. The following ways teenagers see life guide their short-term decisions, fuel risk-taking, and inflict injury on them and their future families.

Unfortunately, emerging adults believe they owe it to themselves to question what they have been taught for the greater good of discovering themselves in the process. To maintain all their religious upbringing, without critical questioning, is perceived as a form of self-betrayal to discovering personal identity through a multitude of "enjoyable and interesting experiences."[8] Failing to distinguish their view of the world from their parents', they feel, undermines self-discovery, independence from parents, and thinking for themselves.[9]

To what extent will emerging adults go to find themselves? Serial relationships, many including sex, serve the individual's quest for identity rather than being a biblical expression of identity stability and self-sacrificing love for another person.[10]

Marriage is indefinitely set aside for fear that it will narrowly restrict the individual's potential for a variety of relationship experiences in which they might find themselves and their soul mate.[11] Along the way, men and women hurt, use, and discard one another in the name of this quest. The end result is that the adult characteristics necessary for future healthy marriages, such as putting others first, exclusivity, and commitment remain undeveloped.[12]

Emerging Adults and Readiness for Marriage

Now for some good news. The future could be quite different from the present. Parenting approaches described in this book could lead to emerging adults prepared to make solid marriage commitments in the years soon after high school. In the not-too-distant future:

- Those who marry around 22, when formal education sometimes ends, might miss much of the emotional and spiritual scarring that takes place between that age and the average ages of 27 or 28.

- Those who find God's mate and experience His leadership could be well prepared to marry even before completing vocational school, military service, or college. Newly married couples could then complete their education and other commitments with the same motivation and tenaciousness as singles (and perhaps more).

These thoughts seem strange in the current culture. Can parents actually prepare their offspring to form lifetime marriages in their younger 20s? As noted in chapter 2, marriages in the biblical period often involved those we now call teenagers. Just a century or two ago, parents prepared their children to marry at 16 or 17, and divorce was very rare.

The messages of this book are not:

- We need to get young people to marry quickly just so they won't have so much sex.

- All people should marry right after high school.

Instead, the messages are:

- In the power of the Spirit, parents can accelerate preparation for marriage during the teenage years. Then offspring can be ready to marry whenever they find God's person and God's leadership, whether that is at age 20 or 50. The goal is a marriage with the longevity and gospel-drenched characteristics described in the Bible.

- Those who unnecessarily delay marriage beyond God's schedule develop a blend of physical, relational, and spiritual complications that threaten lasting, satisfying marriages that make spouses and children more like Jesus.

- In the six or seven years between college and marriage, many emerging adults develop relationship patterns that permanently alter the likelihood of failed or dysfunctional marriages.

College Finances

If you always planned to provide financial support for training or college, you can affirm godly unions during college by continuing to provide that basic support after marriage. A direct payment to an institution to apply to tuition, with no other financial entanglements, can leave newlyweds free to build an independent home and marriage together.

Parents in the past often feared their offspring were not mature enough to continue college or training after getting married. So those parents felt they had to threaten their student with, "If you get married now, we are going to cut you off."

In the future parents who have parented specifically in the direction of maturity may have less fear about shortsighted decisions. They may choose to continue to invest financially since they are confident wise decisions will be made about continuing education.

The Timing of Marriage

Why do men and women wait until the average ages of 28 and 26, respectively? Does anyone think that preparations really take this long? This delay is unnecessary if parents accelerate preparation for marriage during the teenage years. Marrying God's person in God's timing, whenever that might be, can lead to lasting, Christ-honoring marriages with full families.

When will emerging adults begin to say, "Enough's enough! I've found 'me;' I'm capable of being independent and responsible, and now I'm ready to commit to someone else in marriage"? They will say so when they feel ready, either because you have prepared them or after 10 plus years of scarring experimentation.

Surprisingly, some emerging adults believe marriage is sacred and enduring and should not be entered lightly. Rather than subject their family to the pain of future divorce, they choose to endure the devastating pain[13] of "serial monogamy"[14]—repeated failed relationships before marriage. You can guide your teenager to believe that marriages that take place on God's schedule, even in the younger 20s, can be lasting.

Too many emerging adults *feel* ready for marriage "when they are done being single"[15] and enjoying the comforts and conveniences of no- commitment relationships.[16] This contrasts with the young (Prov. 5:18; Mal. 2:14), selfless (Eph. 5:25–33) marriages described in the Bible. The result of these perceptions of readiness is unnecessary marriage delay.

You can develop in your teenagers many features of marriage readiness as you coach, teach, and model life before them.[17] Some readiness characteristics can't be attained without independent adult experiences. But you can lay the groundwork for such readiness as you deposit with them your knowledge and wisdom. Undergirding the characteristics essential for marriage with clear guidance from Scripture will prepare your teenagers for healthy and productive adulthood.

Emerging Adults and Hollow Religion

Many Christian parents have hedged their bets that weekly attendance at church will form a protective morality force field around their offspring in emerging adulthood. Research, however, shows that church attendance alone actually has little to do with critical decisions made concerning identity, sexuality, relationships and marriage,[18] or even their own religious beliefs.[19]

The number one indicator of the nature of faith of emerging adults is the nature of the faith of their parents.[20] This theme will be amplified in chapter 8. But for now, here is some good news. If you have an authentic, growing, gospel-immersed relationship with Jesus, you are taking important steps toward building and reinforcing a faith in your offspring that can withstand the bombardments of emerging adulthood.

Emerging Adults and the Allure of the World

You can acknowledge to your teenager that the world *does* have *something* to offer. There are glimmers of glory in creation many find worthy of worship (Rom. 1). It is incorrect to think that only Christians can experience the graces of creation (Matt. 5:45). A man and a woman are created to care for each other, share life together, know each other deeply and intimately, and sexually delight in each other. Two become one. The "not-goodness" of loneliness becomes the "very goodness" of companionship. Friendship, laughter, intimacy, compassion, pleasure, and love are soul-piercing sparkles of God's glory accessible to anyone.

Emerging adults always will choose the glory play—the glory of the thrill, the glory of relationship, or the glory of beauty. Think about it. If the delights of sexual intimacy had no glory, 95 percent of people wouldn't have premarital sex at great risk to their souls, bodies, relationships, and futures. The longing for the glory of human, flesh- and-blood intimacy is a deeply felt and terribly powerful yearning implanted by God.

It is a mistake to risk the moral behavior of the Christian emerging adult on the false hope that the world has no glory to offer. It does. But you can proclaim to your offspring an exceedingly superior glory that gives biblical focus and context to what God implanted within.

The Practical Gospel

Some parents have been led to believe that moral imperatives, communication skills, and conflict-resolution strategies are the quick remedies adequate to prepare teenagers for marriage. While those things are helpful, only a perspective that flows from the gospel has the power to create and sustain God-honoring marriages. Only the gospel deposes unworthy heart masters that fundamentally wreck marriages.

What Is the Gospel?

The gospel (good news) is that, though undeserved, Jesus lived perfectly, died sinlessly, and rose victoriously to secure our rescue. Second Corinthians 5:21 says that He became our sin so that we could literally become His righteousness. When we receive that grace in faith and repentance, then He fully accepts us.

This rescue has eternal implications. But the gospel also matters in terms of the rubber-meets-the-road daily grind of marriage. Your teenagers grasping the glory of Jesus is at the heart of their finding love and living happily ever after.

King of Glory

Lest the glory of King Jesus sound too abstract, consider what is factually going on in heaven right this second. Seated at the right hand of God the

Father is Jesus Christ, the Anointed Son. Imposing angels encircle the throne crying out "Holy, Holy, Holy" and "Worthy, Worthy, Worthy" to the Lamb of God. God has directed the worship and subjugation of all creation, people, and galaxies alike to direct their worship and allegiance to Jesus the Son, the Name above all names.

Who is like this? Who is the universe's center of attention? Who radiates such glory? When I consider the lesser things that I put on the throne of my heart, I am embarrassed for Jesus. When I put my comfort and happiness, intimacy itself, or possessions on the throne, I am declaring that I belong on my heart's throne. Only One is worthy of worship and can satisfy my, and every emerging adult's, indwelling desire for glory.

Creation's glimpses of glory become magnified and purified when experienced under the reign of glorious King Jesus. More than that, we experience more than just *glimpses* of glory. We experience the *fountainhead* of glory Himself! Our lives are freed to live for Him, deeply and most intimately satisfied in the eternal, limitless glory of our Creator "who richly supplies us with all things to enjoy" (1 Tim. 6:17).

Paul compared the glory of the Creator to the glory of the created and counted "all things to be loss in view of the surpassing value of knowing Christ Jesus my Lord, for whom I have suffered the loss of all things, and count them but rubbish so that I may gain Christ" (Phil. 3:8).

Rescuer King

When the King of heaven deposes the inferior kings of our hearts, we have the hope of becoming who we were made by Him to become (identity). He rescues us from ourselves that we might also experience the deepest, purest, most satisfying companionship—first vertically and also horizontally (intimacy). Any preparation for marriage must be rooted in the gospel so that Jesus can rescue our hearts from self-rule and can rescue our marriages as well.

The gospel begins and ensures teenagers' progressive subordination to Christ in every area of their lives. For marriage and future families to work, your teenager must hold to the unshakeable foundation of one man and one woman who are progressively being remade by Jesus Christ. The gospel alone holds the answer to our teenagers' becoming new creations controlled by the Spirit as they move toward adulthood.

Purpose of Marriage

Something and someone is shaping your child's vision of what marriage is supposed to look like. All visions for marriage are not equally valid. When he or she steps out of the protection of your home as an emerging adult, the vision your teenager has formed, right or wrong, will drive many decisions leading up to, and in, marriage.[21] Is the purpose of marriage to not be alone, to be in love, to enjoy harmony with a soul mate, or to start a family?

The purpose of marriage begins with God at creation. God provided Adam with Eve to fulfill a life purpose that was best fulfilled together. He created the marriage relationship to be unique among all other relationships—unique in support, commitment, total intimacy, and longevity.

For teenagers today that original goal of rightly relating to the Creator has been made possible by the gospel. They are reconciled to God and are redeemed to pursue the goals of treasuring Christ, becoming like Him, and making Him known. Marriage provides an irreplaceable expression of God's transforming grace, in terms of oneness, transformation, and legacy.

Oneness

The oneness afforded by marriage points to the complete intimacy and delight found in union with Christ. "Biblical writers use the marriage metaphor to depict the legal, deeply personal, two-sided nature of the believer's relationship to God" in Christ.[22]

The purpose of the believer is to treasure Christ above all else. Marriage provides opportunity for spouses to help and complement each other in fulfilling that purpose. Only two believers can experience the deepest unity as they treasure Christ together and move forward with a shared life purpose.

Transformation

Marriage provides a unique context for spiritual transformation. As a man and woman pursue the pure worship of God in their individual lives, the marriage partner is to assist that. No discipleship context requires greater depth of rescue than marriage—it exposes the remaining hold of sin and self that constantly battles for the heart's throne. Godly marriage requires a depth of death to self and dependence on Christ that brings about Christlike transformation.

Legacy

Marriage is meant to make a difference. The way husbands and wives treat each other clarifies or confuses the gospel of Christ's undeserved, self-sacrificial love for the family's children and the watching world.

The family is meant to be a discipleship center where the gospel becomes firmly rooted in spouses and children. It is to leave a legacy of missions and ministry in this generation, both locally and globally. It is likewise meant to impact the world through raising godly offspring who treasure Christ and take the gospel of His grace to the ends of the earth in their own generation.

What might those three biblical marriage purposes look like in a purpose statement?

> The purpose of our marriage is to treasure and
> become like Jesus together, to proclaim His gospel of love
> in our marriage relationship and to the ends of the earth,
> and to replicate this purpose in a new generation.

Use any wording you like, but help your teenager understand the biblical purposes of oneness, transformation, and legacy. Such a vision for marriage will preclude entanglements with those unable to fulfill God's design for marriage.

Marriage Expectations

"This is not the man I married!"
But of course, he is. He is precisely the man she married.
It's the guy she dated who was the fake![23]

Gospel-Balanced Expectations

Every marriage partner enters into marriage expecting his or her spouse, and married life, to be a certain way. This is unavoidable. Sometimes a spouse's dreams, desires, or wants become unrealistic demands.[24] Other times couples are simply not anticipating the kinds of normal challenges and adjustments most marriages face. Poor adjustments to expectation letdowns can quickly become painful and even jeopardize the marriage.

Preparing teenagers for marriage involves giving them a gospel framework for dealing with unmet expectations. A teenager should anticipate that indwelling sin makes the following marriage contributions.

- You and your spouse struggle with sin and self.

- Your spouse, or the marriage itself, is unable to make you happy, but you want it to.

- You feel misunderstood and wronged and aren't sure how to move past this point.

Typical, difficult marriage scenarios amplify the condition of the heart.

- Your spouse handles situations and people far differently from you or your parents.

- You have different approaches to making and spending money, gender roles, family scheduling, affection and intimacy, and parenting.

- You enter into sexual intimacy from different relationship and emotional histories.

- Gender and personality differences affect how you give and receive love, respect, and honor.[25]

Tell your teenager the gospel proclaims hope that Jesus not only saves us for eternity but rescues us from being mastered by self and thereby wrecking our marriages. There is no room for selfishness and spiritual immaturity in thriving marriages. "We are to grow up in all aspects into Him who is the head, even Christ" (Eph. 4:15). When we humbly recognize our own struggles with sin and the challenges of marriage, we grow in patience, compassion, and grace with our partner.

Your teenager needs to know that gospel-remedy commitments foster marriage joy and stability. You might use the following outline for some focused conversations.

- Anchor your marriage and family on the truths and application of God's Word.

- Take responsibility; the problem is the sin within you and your spouse.

- Turn to Jesus Christ for the desire and ability obedience requires.

- Remove the burden from your spouse to deeply satisfy you as only Christ can—then become satisfied in Christ.

- Recognize the differences in your spouse are not necessarily sinful. Appreciate them.

- Forgive and work through big and small things quickly.[26]

- Pray with, serve, and encourage one another toward spiritual growth.

- Choose to relate nonverbally, verbally, affectionately, and sexually in the self-giving love defined by Scripture and empowered by the Spirit.

Gospel-Defined Love

Teenagers intuitively know that marriage should be about love. But not all understand the love of God clearly enough to extend it to a spouse or other family member. Counselor and relationship expert, Paul Tripp, uses 1 John 4 to clarify the fourfold love of God in this way:

- Love is willing self-sacrifice

- for the good of another

- that does not require reciprocation

- or that the other person is deserving.[27]

Christian marriages are to display this kind of love. This is highlighted in Ephesians 5:25–33. "As Christ loved the church," husbands are to love their wives sacrificially. Understanding and applying biblical love can make shelves of marriage-help books irrelevant and unnecessary. The gospel is the answer to the self-absorbed condition of the human heart. The gospel not only defines love but also makes it possible by the transformation of grace.

The gospel does another important thing. It exposes nonlove. Much of what emerging adults call love is really self-love. We worship the feelings of being loved and cherished by another. We don't love the person; we love being loved. "His grace rescues you from your obsession with self-love and welcomes you to the joyous work of loving another."[28]

Gospel-Purified Sexuality

Teenagers also need to understand that sexual decisions now will affect the ability of both spouses completely to enjoy satisfying sex in marriage. Early sexual experiences (especially those involving orgasm) rewire the brain, misshape the heart, and impact all future relationships.

A study of more than 29,000 university adults showed that over two-thirds of emerging adults engage in five or more hours of weekly pornography. Pornography decreases sexual fulfillment by conditioning the body to desire and respond mainly to stimuli not present in real marriage and to expect sexual fulfillment on demand.[29]

Consider some other research findings related to early sex:

- For many, sexual experiences begin at 13, and with the average marriage age of 28, they rack up 15 years of guilt and dysfunction.[30]

- 70% of all emerging adults live with regret, having underestimated the toll on emotions and subsequent guilt.[31] Some carry emotional wounds that inhibit their ability to feel or have empathy toward others.[32]

- Many realize how "profound and precious" sex is only after it's too late.[33]

On the other hand, gospel-purified sexuality:

- Places sexual sin *and* shame on Christ so we bear it no more.

- Progressively cures us of the selfishness that provokes out-of-bounds sexuality.

- Frees us from the unwillingness and inability to "learn to control your own body in a way that is holy and honorable" (1 Thess. 4:4, NIV) prior to, and after, marriage.

- Gives us grace to help us draw wise boundaries that protect our spouse and marriage.

- Provides a spirit of understanding and honor for a spouse's gender differences.[34]

- Provides pure and loving character by which sexuality can be the context of real love and intimacy rather than selfish release.

You are critical in preparing your teenager to handle the treasure of sexuality through the hope of the gospel. Only the gospel preaches God's standards along with the corresponding grace to be truly righteous. Moore urges parents to help their teen establish, mark, and defend their boundaries using a chart of progressing physical intimacy.[35] This type of preparation strategy is a huge leap in the right direction for parents. Such conversations are critical.

But remember, your conversations should be infused with the gospel. Too often, the few parents and churches with the fortitude to handle the sexuality issue do so out of a morality framework, which provides nothing more than reasons for holiness standards without the power of the gospel to attain them.

Gospel-Responsible Communication

"What is the source of quarrels and conflicts among you? Is not the source your pleasures that wage war in your members?" (James 4:1). Teenagers and emerging adults ready to marry in God's timing will understand the gospel's radical effect on communication. Careless communication can quickly wound hearts, erode marriages, and dishonor the Lord and people.

Responsible communication allows the exchange of thoughts, feelings, commitments, praise, and service. This is why the Bible so clearly marks out the manner and method of communication that denies self, glorifies God, and fortifies marriages.

Good communication builds trust, unity, intimacy, and stability between couples little by little over time.[36] One critical way to prepare your teenager for adult family relationships is by modeling and expecting honoring communication among all family members now. Your home can reveal God's grace by the graceful interactions between each of its members. There is no room for words that tear down or fail to build up spouses, siblings, parents, and children.

The following outline can help you plan focused conversations with your teenager:

- Foster mutual understanding (1 Pet. 3:7) by sending and receiving messages accurately through active listening.

- Provide a safe and authentic climate of communication. "Intimacy and connection become natural by-products of their freedom to be authentic with one another."[37]

- "Speak the truth in love" (Eph. 4:15). The manner of gospel-infused communication takes on the character of Christ's love and is empowered by the Spirit. Love tells the truth with the kindness, gentleness, and patience of the indwelling, controlling Spirit of God Himself (Gal. 5:22).

- Be angry without sinning against other people. The gospel provides hope for God-honoring behavior when emotions run high.

- Humbly and quickly ask for forgiveness when walking in the flesh produces fleshly responses.

Gospel Boundaries

Every marriage committed to live out its God-ordained purpose must have boundaries. Boundaries are the restrictions adopted by couples taking responsibility for their marriage.[38] They are formed to protect a marriage from the consequences of out-of-bounds behavior and unruly hearts. Teenagers need to understand critical marriage boundaries before entering emerging adulthood.

Gospel-Bound Permanence

Permanence is a gospel boundary. The gospel preaches that the love and faithfulness of God is unconditional and permanent. Believers are called to display the gospel in the marriage relationship; the marriage must tell the truth about God.[39] Therefore, the marriage must never go outside of the boundary of permanence into the land of sexual unfaithfulness or divorce. This treacherously violates the clear will of God for marriages to honor God, each other, and to produce godly offspring (Mal. 2:14–15).

To glorify Christ and to give your children a godly example:

- Refuse to entertain thoughts of a soul mate other than your spouse. You may encounter other believers who are more physically beautiful, emotionally attentive, and verbally affirming than your spouse. God makes beautiful people more and more beautiful. But never mistake the attractiveness of another person, even if accompanied by an emotional spark, as a sign of God's approval to cross this boundary.

- Build an impassable barricade with the gospel. Refuse to get close to a rival in any way for the sake of your marriage, God's glory, and your children. Walk down opposite hallways. Minimize eye contact. Ride in another carpool.

- Receive God's grace that is eager to return your heart to pure faithfulness and sanity. Someday your teenager likely will follow your example.

Gospel-Bound Priority

One of the greatest dangers for marriages is when good third parties take priority over your spouse. You can equip your teenager to understand threats to making a spouse a priority:

- Children, parents, friends, and even church are eager to get the attention and energy your spouse is entitled to.

- A lifestyle of yes to everything and everyone else is inevitably a lifestyle of no to your marriage.

- A pace of activity that doesn't leave room to nurture oneness, transformation, and legacy is serving a master that is not Jesus Christ. The gospel stands ready to rescue you from this tyrant.

- You honor your spouse by growing in biblical wisdom about marriage. This will mean seeking godly wisdom from gospel-saturated marriage resources, engaging equipping opportunities initiated by your church, conversations with pastoral staff, and sometimes professional Christian counselors.

Gospel-Bound Resources

This may seem out of place in a chapter on marriage, but money management is a magnet for marriage difficulties. The boundary of gospel-bound resources is a call to stay within the limits of God's provision. You can train children as soon as they begin any income stream to steward their resources according to God's will. Your teenager needs to know:

- Money should be made ethically.

- A tithe to the local church and generous kingdom giving is normative for Christian families.

- Godly contentment takes away the desire to live beyond your means.

- Debt robs families of spiritual focus by creating pressure for more income by one or both spouses.

- Resources bound by the gospel are funneled back into Great Commission causes. One example is a family missions savings account that will be used to be on mission together.

Couples who ensure their income is governed by the comprehensive rule of King Jesus experience economic and heart freedom. They also experience their needs being met by a Perfect Provider. Through your teaching and your example, that becomes the likely outcome for your teenager someday.

In summary:

- Many emerging adults are charting a course that will end in pain and fractured marriages.

- Teenagers can begin now to establish most preparations for a marriage of God's timing.

- The gospel provides a framework for defining love, adjusting to expectation letdowns, and building critical boundaries.

- Those ready for marriage should understand love, expectations, sexuality, and communication through a gospel lens.

- Those ready for marriage should understand the importance of the boundaries of permanence, priority, and resources in light of the gospel.

CHAPTER 8: PREPARING YOUR TEENAGER TO BE A MATURE BELIEVER

Richard Ross

You can see your teenager leave home with a vibrant faith that will last a lifetime.

You really do want what is best for your child. You want your child to grow into a responsible adult. You want to see your child able to earn a living and to see his or her dreams fulfilled. You want your child to live in rich adult relationships and perhaps have a loving family. You want your child to be moral and to be a responsible citizen. You want your child to be happy. But the question is:

> What do you want to see more than
> anything when your child is an adult?

Patrick Lencioni consults with Fortune 500 companies related to core values, strategies, and objectives. As a husband and father, it dawned on him that he could apply some of the thinking from his consulting business to life with his own family. The positive results have prompted him to invite other parents to follow his lead.

Lencioni challenges parents to determine the core values for their families. He says, "The key to identifying your core values is realizing that you should have just two or three, and that all the good qualities under the sun—as wonderful and desirable as they might be—are not necessarily good candidates to be called core for your family."[1]

Of all the values you embrace, what are the two or three that rise to the top? What goals do you have for your children that trump all others? Tim Kimmel notes:

> The standard mistake Christian parents make is concentrating their efforts on raising children who grow up to be *successful*. The problem with this plan is that it's already dead-on-arrival spiritually because of how our culture

quantifies success. The standard measurements for success are wealth, beauty, power, and fame. . . . What Christian parents don't seem to realize is that God places no special value on wealth, beauty, power, and fame in the Bible. These four goals have no bearing on whether or not a child will . . . have any eternal impact.[2]

Parents who are transformed children of God choose core values consistent with who He is, what He has said in His Word, and what He does. They choose core values that flow out of the desires God has for each of their children:

1. Redeemed by faith into a relationship with Christ.

2. Living as a maturing believer.

3. Fulfilling the specific mission he or she has been given on earth.

Redemption

Nothing in parenting matters more than where your own children will spend forever and ever. Since the ultimate purpose of every person is to glorify the Father, the beginning place is faith in His Son Jesus Christ.

For parents the stakes are too high to leave teaching your kids about eternity with others. While the following lines can help you prepare to talk with your teenager about this life-or-death matter, be affirmed in this—God loves your kids and wants them to love Him more than you do. And God wants to equip you to live your life of faith before your kids in such a way that they will want to know God.

Praying for your kids to come to know Christ as Lord and Savior is not a new idea. But it is only an idea unless you really pray. Scripture says, "For our struggle is not against flesh and blood, but against the rulers, against the powers, against the world forces of this darkness, against the spiritual forces of wickedness in the heavenly places" (Eph. 6:12). Praying for your kids is important.

The Holy Spirit gives power to the words of Scripture. Read each passage below as you share more of Christ with your teenager.

- The Bible says there is only one way to heaven (John 14:6).

- Good works cannot save you (Eph. 2:8–9).

Share your own struggles with trying to be "good enough" for God and how you have realized this is not what God desires. Share your own joy and wonder at what God has done for you through Jesus and how much you love Him for it.

To trust Jesus Christ, here is what you must do:

- Admit you are a sinner (Rom. 3:23; 5:12; 1 John 1:10).

- Be willing to turn from sin (repent) and turn toward Jesus (Luke 13:5; Acts 17:30).

- Believe that Jesus Christ died for you, was buried, and rose from the dead (John 3:16; Rom. 5:8; 10:9).

- Through prayer invite Christ to be both Savior and Master (Rom. 10:10, 13).

A Sample Prayer: "Dear God, I am a sinner and need forgiveness. I believe Jesus Christ shed His precious blood, dying on a cross, and rose from the dead. I believe His death was the payment for my sins that I might be rightly related to God. I am willing to turn from sin and discover real life in relationship with You. I now invite Christ to come into my heart and life as my personal Savior and Lord."

Realize this decision is only the beginning. Questions and doubts will come. Be ready and respond with grace. Pray often for your teenager to be rooted in the truth of the gospel.

Living as a Maturing Believer

Once a child comes to know Christ, guiding that child toward being a maturing believer is the highest priority. Living as a maturing believer has many facets.

Love for God

The Father created your child because He deeply desires to have a relationship with that child. Your child exists to share ever-increasing love, closeness, and fellowship with the One who Jesus called Abba, which means Daddy. Your child increasingly can love God even as awe of His power and holiness deepens.

According to Scripture, the first and greatest commandment for believers is to love God with all one's heart, soul, mind, and strength. Pastor J. D. Greear says, "God desires a people who desire Him, who serve Him because they love Him. . . . Spiritual giftedness, doctrinal mastery, audacious faith, and radical obedience do not equal the only thing that actually matters to God—love for Him. Without love even the most radical devotion to God is of no value to Him."[3]

Almost every teenager at church believes in God. Many would say they try to obey God. But only a handful truthfully could say they find delight in their relationship with Abba Father. The others do not know what they are missing.

Teenagers love God because they find great joy in who He is. The result of more deeply loving Him is their transformation into the image of His Son. Scot McKnight says, "When we genuinely love God with all of our hearts, all of our souls, all of our minds, and all of our strength, this sacred love will transform our speech, convert our actions, and inspire our worship."[4]

We have the privilege of inviting teenagers constantly to abide in Christ. According to Greear, the Greek word for "abide,", *meno*, means: "literally 'to make your home in.' When we 'make our home in' His love—feeling it, saturating ourselves with it, reflecting on it, standing in awe of it—spiritual fruit begins to spring up naturally from us like roses on a rose bush."[5]

Crucial questions for every parent are:

> Does my daughter love God with all of her being?
> Will my son love God with all his being
> through all his days as an adult?

Gratitude for Grace and the Gospel

You cannot announce to our teenager, "Your Divine Lover commands you to love Him, so you better obey that command this week." Instead, you guide your teenager to embrace the wonder and the beauty of the gospel—knowing that will awaken a heart of love.

Greear says: "The Spirit of God uses the beauty of the gospel to awaken in our hearts a desire for God. 'We love Him,' the apostle John would say, 'because He first loved us' (1 John 4:19, NKJV). Love for God grows out of an experience of the love of God."[6]

Tim Kimmel adds, "God desires to have an intimate relationship with people. He primarily creates and maintains that relationship through the qualities and character of His grace. Regardless of a person's condition, God can do marvelous things in, on, for, and through him or her when that person allows Him to turn him or her into living extensions of His heart of grace."[7] When we lead our kids to abide (make their life) in Christ, He does amazing things through them.

Your teenager's love for God will increase as your teenager becomes more and more aware of the love of God. Your teenager's gratitude to God will increase as your teenager comes to understand the marvelous grace of God. (Grace is mercy given by God because He desires to give it, not because of anything believers have done to earn it.) For the teenager, grasping the miracle of grace and forgiveness opens the door to loving gratitude.

Kimmel notes, "If someone . . . asked me to unpack a philosophy, strategy, and tactics for transferring a passionate heart for Jesus to the next generation, I'd write out something like this: 'I want to connect to the heart of my child in such a way that I condition them to have a tender heart for God. I'll do this through the power of God's grace!'"[8]

The Supreme Majesty of Christ

Most church teenagers know and love Jesus. They really do. But most tend to know Him as a friend and not much more.

Worst case, some teenagers may see Jesus as their little buddy who rides with them in their shirt pocket. He is always there in case they need to pull Him out to "poof" some difficulty away. But the problem is, teenagers may believe He can be returned to their pocket—conveniently out of sight and out of mind—until needed again.

If teenagers today primarily know Jesus as a friend who gives gifts, where do you think they got that idea? Is it possible they have grown up surrounded by Christian adults who also embrace Christ for His benefits, a Christ who is too small?

Worshipping a small Jesus who is not the real Jesus is idolatry. Parents must understand the full scope of who Jesus is and then communicate that effectively to their teenagers. Failing to do so is setting teenagers up to fail to understand Him.

When the Son had made purification of sins on the cross, He ascended to heaven and was enthroned at the right hand of the Majesty on high. The Father announced that in this age of the church, God the Son is to have supremacy.

But in the U.S., in the 1960s things began to go wrong. Believers generally shifted their primary focus to becoming more prosperous, comfortable, and happy. They still held to Jesus but just as their church mascot and an addendum to pursuing the American dream.

Believers still speak of Jesus but mostly concerning the days He walked on earth. They are more likely to picture Him sitting on a big rock with giggling children in His lap than reigning from the throne of heaven. Sermons, Bible lessons, and church hallway conversations are almost completely devoid of any focus on the transcendent majesty of who the Son is today.

Do you believe Christ will be more glorious than we can imagine on the day of His return? Do you think believers will be wonderfully overwhelmed when they see Him split open the heavens and descend to earth? Absorb this thought: Who Christ will be that day is precisely who He is today. Precisely. In your prayer time this morning, is that how you saw Him in your mind's eye? Did your awe of Him cause you to spend more time praising and adoring Him than making requests of Him?

Your own awakening to Christ can splash over onto all your children. From time to time you can ask yourself, Are my children encountering a larger vision of Christ and His supreme majesty because they live in my home?

Transformed More into the Image of Christ

Children who are maturing as believers will come to look more and more like Jesus. They will carry more of His aroma on their lives now and into adulthood.

Norman Wright says: "What is the purpose of the new self? It's Godlikeness. Paul told the Colossians, '[You] have put on the new self, which is being renewed in knowledge in the image of its Creator' (Col. 3:10). Now, you and I and each of your children are to be like Jesus. He was God made human. Isn't it interesting and amazing that He became like us so we might become like Him."[9]

Romans 12:2 says, "Be transformed by the renewing of your mind." "The word 'transformed' in Romans 12 comes from an English word 'metamorphosis.' John Ortberg offers the best definition of morphing: 'When morphing happens, I don't just do the things Jesus would have done; I find myself wanting to do them. They appeal to me. They make sense. I don't just go around trying to do right things; I become the right sort of person.'"[10]

The Coming of Christ's Kingdom on Earth

A maturing teenage believer invites Christ to live His powerful life through him in order to see the kingdom come more on the earth.

> You do not challenge your child to live *for* Christ, but you guide your child to invite Christ to live *through* him or her.

What God wants to do is live through your son or daughter to accomplish His purposes. He brings both the purpose and the power to accomplish what He desires. Their response is to submit to Him. Leading your kids to understand this will enable them to die daily to their own selfishness and embrace the larger greatness of Christ's kingdom.

Scripture records more than 90 references Christ made to His kingdom (His rule and reign). In the Model Prayer, Jesus prays, "Our Father who is in heaven, Hallowed be Your name. Your kingdom come. Your will be done, on earth as it is in heaven" (Matt. 6:9–10).

Nothing can stop King Jesus, and thus nothing can stop the growth of the kingdom. He allows believers to join Him in kingdom activity, but He is not dependent on us for that activity.

Duty and obligation are poor motivators. Gratitude for grace is far, far more powerful. Do your children share sentiments similar to these? "Having . . . been found by Him, and overwhelmed by His grace, my heart is growing in love for Him and others. . . . I think about myself less now than I ever have—mainly because I have found a greater, more captivating kingdom to live for than my own. The splendor of His kingdom has made me bored with mine."[11]

So, how do we get teenagers who embrace kingdom activity out of hearts of gratitude for grace? Primarily, we give them heart connections with other believers who have exuberant gratitude for grace. Transformed friends are part of the answer, but even more important are parents and youth leaders who joyfully are responding to all that Christ has done.

Counting All as Loss for Christ's Surpassing Greatness

When teenagers and adults begin to figure out who Christ really is today, they fall before Him and shout, "Holy, Holy, Holy!" They are overwhelmed and in awe. As they grasp more and more of His greatness, then it makes perfect sense to count everything else as loss.

Paul declares, "But whatever things were gain to me, those things I have counted as loss for the sake of Christ. More than that, I count all things to be loss in view of the surpassing value of knowing Christ Jesus my Lord, for whom I have suffered the loss of all things, and count them but rubbish so that I may gain Christ" (Phil. 3:7–8).

Timothy Keller calls the heart an idol factory. The heart takes good things like family and possessions and turns them into ultimate things. Our heart deifies them as the center of life. They begin to absorb more of our heart and imagination than God.[12] This is why "have no other gods before Me" is the first commandment.

Use your imagination. Picture a generation of teenagers who love Christ with all their heart, soul, mind, and strength. Picture teenagers who adore the King above relationships, possessions, comfort, and a long life—who absolutely would lay those things down at Christ's command. Picture teenagers who are not bound to the culture. A generation such as that can—quite literally—change the world.

Your offspring will not likely be called to martyrdom for the sake of the gospel. But it is important they let Christ know they would consider it a high honor to do so. Jesus said, "The hour has come for the Son of Man to be glorified. Truly, truly, I say to you, unless a grain of wheat falls into the earth and dies, it remains alone; but if it dies, it bears much fruit. He who loves his life loses it, and he who hates his life in this world will keep it to life eternal" (John 12:23–25).

Counting all loss for His surpassing greatness opens the door for Christ to live His powerful life through parents and teenagers. In His strength they can then complete their mission on earth, which will bring great glory to God. And that happens to be the reason for existence.

Fulfilling One's Specific Mission on the Earth

How would your teenager answer these questions: Why do you exist? What is your purpose on planet Earth? Such questions are important. Christian teenagers can make solid decisions about the future when they begin to have some answers.

Of course, purpose in life is not somehow unique to being a teenager. From a biblical perspective, children, teenagers, and senior adults have the same purpose. God says, "I will say to the north, 'Give them up!' And to the south, 'Do not hold them back.' Bring My sons from afar and My daughters from the ends of the earth, everyone who is called by My name, and whom I have created for My glory, whom I have formed, even whom I have made" (Isa. 43:6–7). People were created and now exist for His glory.

What if your teenager really came to believe that? What if a real desire for God's glory became the basis for decisions? This would be the polar opposite of "It's all about me." Imagine your teenager saying, God does not exist for me; I exist for His great glory and to make His name more famous on the earth.

David Platt says it this way:

- "The will of God is for you and me to give our lives urgently and recklessly to making the gospel and the glory of God known among all peoples. . . .

- "Will we risk everything—our comfort, our possessions, our safety, our security, our very lives—to make the gospel known among unreached peoples?

- "Such rising up and such risk taking are the unavoidable, urgent results of a life that is radically abandoned to Jesus."[13]

Teenagers need to know the general life purpose they share with all people—to glorify God. They also need to know how to discover God's unique will as they move toward a life of glorifying God as adults.

The first step, of course, is falling even more in love with Jesus. Knowing Christ always precedes knowing His will.

Closely related is walking in whatever light one has of His will today. Scripture says, "In all your ways acknowledge Him, and He will make your paths straight" (Prov. 3:6). Doing God's will today generally leads to discovering more of God's plan for tomorrow. God rarely gives believers the whole picture with specifics regarding the future.

Parents fulfill a large part of their reason for being on earth as they guide their children to be redeemed by faith into a relationship with Christ, living as maturing believers, and fulfilling the specific mission they have been given on earth.

The Spiritual Leadership of Parents

For good or ill, parents make more of a difference in the spiritual development of teenagers than anyone. They do not make just a little bit more of a difference but a great deal more of a difference. This fact has been documented by Christian Smith, Kenda Dean, Kara Powell, Jim Burns, Mark DeVries, David Kinnaman, Rob Rienow, Brian Haynes, Mark Holman, and a host of other researchers and writers.

The National Study of Youth and Religion confirmed what many researchers suspected. Who parents are basically is who teenagers will become.[14] The question is not whether parents will have influence. The question is whether that influence will lead teenagers to live in awe of God's Son and long for His kingdom to come on earth.

Speaking as a parent, researcher David Kinnaman says: "Not only do we tend to expect too little of our young people, we expect too little of ourselves, and those low expectations spill over onto our students. If faith in Christ is not shaping every facet of our lives, transforming us into people who love God with heart, soul, mind, and body (see Luke 10:27), why would we expect more from the next generation?"[15]

Transparency

The more spiritually vibrant and alive the parents are, the more this will overflow onto their children. And the more transparent parents are about their own spiritual journey, the more their teenagers will tend to follow in similar directions.

Parents who make conversations about faith more intentional tend to use lots of questions. Questions have a place, but teenagers need to hear mom and dad talk about their walk with Christ, their love for Him, their discoveries about Him in Scripture, and ways they have joined Him in His kingdom activity. And they need to share ways they have seen God at work. Brian Haynes calls these God sightings.

It is powerful when parents say things similar to:

- "I've been looking forward to breakfast because I want to tell you what the Holy Spirit showed me in Scripture this morning."

- "In my prayer time this morning, I almost felt as if Abba Father had His mighty arms around me."

- "I love King Jesus with all of my heart."

Modeling. Everyone enjoys a good movie based on a best-selling novel. Consider an analogy. Picture the Bible as the book—the novel. The movie based on the Bible is the daily lives of parents. Parents have the great privilege and the great responsibility to unfold for their children the intriguing drama of real life in Christ. They turn the truth of Scripture into high-definition video that is easy for their children to absorb.

Intentional spiritual practices in the home are important. They are biblical and they impact lives. But research says that the running movie—life lived out by the parent—has as much or even more impact than the intentional practices.

Heart Connections and Spiritual Influence

Your call from God and unique position in your children's lives give you, by far, the greatest influence with them. Your children will tend to delight in embracing your faith if they share heart connections with you. Why? Teenagers who are loved by their parents with the warm love of Christ (Eph. 5:22-6:4) more easily embrace Christ Himself as His Spirit calls them into relationship.

Parents who keep heart connections warm and strong usually see visible evidence their faith and values are passing to their children. "And he will turn the hearts of fathers to their children and the hearts of children to their fathers" (Mal. 4:6, HCSB).

A heart connection is the "pipeline" that connects the hearts of the parent and teen. Through that pipeline of warm relationships, spiritual impact flows from one generation to the next.

Too little quality time together or emotional injury can damage heart connections. If you and your teen grow distant from each other, the pipe is pulled loose. The probability is that you then will have little spiritual impact, even if you teach and live out biblical truth before your teenager.

If your teenager loses a heart connection with you, he or she often will try to fill the void by giving the pipe to peers. Some of those peers, from weak homes, may fill the pipe with faithlessness and confused values. But even then Christ offers hope for healing and restored relationships.

Parents rebuild heart connections by:

- Forgiving teenagers for pain they have caused.

- Asking them for forgiveness as appropriate.

- Moving away from emotional outbursts toward teens.

- Spending focused time together.

- Using words to bless, encourage, and build up.

Modeling kingdom living and teaching the Christian faith supplies the spiritual truth that flows through the "pipe." No pipe—no influence. No modeling—no credibility. No teaching—no truth. When all three are present, the high probability is that your teenager, for the glory of the Father and in the power of the Spirit, will spend a lifetime embracing the full majesty of Christ.

Faith Practices at Home

Prayer. Parents lead at home by praying with and for their children. Teenagers need to hear the depth of a parent's love for them revealed in those prayers. They need to hear how keenly a parent wants to release them to God's call and to see spiritual impact radiating out from their lives.

Prayer any time has value, but parents should recognize that teenagers may be especially open to spiritual things at the beginning or ending of the day. In the words of Deuteronomy 6, this influence comes "when you lie down and when you rise up" (v. 7).

Teenagers often are the most transparent at the end of the day. Parents may find themselves sitting on the edge of their teenager's bed, discussing some of the most important things of life in the dark. Parents must capture these moments. Far too quickly children will be grown and gone, and such opportunities will be over.

The complement to morning and evening prayers is prayer as a running conversation throughout the day. Parents pray multiple times with a teenager in a natural and conversational fashion. Over time teenagers learn to pray at the very moment they are celebrating or grieving or needing God's guidance.

Parents open the Bible and teach their teenagers how to pray. Parents complement teaching times by actually praying out loud with their sons and daughters. Over time parents will see their prayers reflected in the prayers of their offspring.

Parents who model well will:

- Hear more spiritual maturity in their teenager's prayers.

- Hear their teenager asking to be filled by the Holy Spirit of God.

- Notice their teenager is praying more and more prayers of praise and adoration before asking for anything.

- Hear requests move from a focus on "me and mine" to a focus on the glory of God.

- Hear their teenager pray for Christ's kingdom to come on earth in the midst of hard situations rather than just automatically asking that all hard situations go away.

Family worship. Most family prayer and conversations about faith are spontaneous, but some take place at planned times. Some call these planned times family worship, and others call them faith talks. They reflect the words from Deuteronomy 6, "when you sit in your house" (v. 7). Such times usually include longer prayer, worship and praise, and reading and discussing Scripture.

Each family should follow Christ's leadership to know how often to gather for worship. Families just beginning this practice might begin by gathering weekly. Chapter 10 presents ways churches can supply parents with resources useful in planning family worship.

Ministry and evangelism. Parents also plan times for the family to care for others in the name of Christ. In your church, adult groups and the youth group may perform compassion ministries. Even if that is true, there still is great value in caring for others as a family. In fact, some researchers believe that performing acts of service with the family is one of the most powerful discipling experiences any child or teenager can have.

Parents can plan family outings to address injustice, spiritual poverty, or needs that already have touched the heart of a teen. When families engage in serving, teens form permanent mental snapshots that what matters most is not themselves but Christ and His mission of redemptive love to others.

Even more important is the family's role in taking the gospel to those who do not know Christ. The Great Commission propels out families to their neighborhood, state, nation, and world. Spiritually alive families exist to see every person on the block, in the high school, and around the world hear about Jesus.

The Future

Wise parents lead out spiritually with an eye toward the future. For example, you teach your teenager principles to use in interpreting any passage of Scripture. You take the time to do that so he can discover what God has to say today. But you also do that so he will be prepared if God leads him to start a Bible study in his college dorm room.

You lead your daughter to share her faith so she can do so the rest of her life. You give your children a foundation in Christian apologetics and worldview so they can be rock-solid believers for a lifetime. You show your son how to discover the will of God, knowing he may use these principles with a tough decision he is facing as a senior adult.

You invested lots of energy teaching your preschoolers how to feed and dress themselves. But now they are prepared to do that through adulthood. In the same way, now is the time to teach a teenager how to feed himself spiritually and how to make the faith his own.

Actually, God's plan for parenting goes beyond an individual parent and teenager. God is orchestrating entire generations. Just as God desired for generations of Hebrews to bless the nations, God still desires that parents join Him in moving the Christian faith down through all the generations for His grand purposes.

You lead worship with your family because you want God's best for your teenager. But you also lead out because you someday want your adult child to lead your grandchild in worship—and for your grandchild to someday lead worship with your great-grandchild.

Family ministry pioneer Rob Rienow says, "It is easy to become so focused on getting through the day at hand that we seldom consider the big picture of God's calling for parents and grandparents. You have been invited into a multigenerational mission. God created your family to be a discipleship center that will build a legacy of faith for generations to come."[16]

CHAPTER 9: SENDING YOUR TEENAGER ON A GAP-YEAR MISSION TRIP

Richard Ross

You can launch your teenager on an experience that will spread the gospel and will help turn boys and girls into young men and women.

Those 18 to 25 know they are living a brief and unique chapter of their lives. These are the years in between the structure of high school and the coming responsibilities of a permanent job and family. These short years provide an opportunity for a "gap year" experience that can accelerate growth toward adulthood, sharpen future goals, and impact Christ's kingdom.

Concept of a Gap Year

Secular culture views a gap year as time out to travel between life stages. The expression usually relates to a trip that lasts from a few weeks or months to a year. This involves delaying or interrupting college or vocational studies for activities such as traveling, volunteering, or working abroad.

College admissions departments view a gap year as "a year taken between high school and college. During this gap-year, students engage in extra-academic and non-academic courses, language studies, volunteer work, travel, internships, sports and more, all for the purpose of improving themselves and their resumes before going to college."[1]

Every Christian teenager should go on short-term mission projects throughout the teenage years and beyond. But at least once, every student should prayerfully consider the life-altering and kingdom-expanding challenge of going to the front lines of missions for a longer period.

Every church youth group should do mission projects together. But at least once, *all* students need to go without the group to do what God uniquely has called and gifted them to do. Young believers may have more reasons than anyone to go on a gap-year adventure for a summer, a semester, or a year.

Developmentally, emerging adults crave a grand adventure. They are ready to do hard things and go to the hard places. This is the perfect time for an assignment so challenging it requires all they are and all the Spirit supplies.

Accelerated Growth toward Adulthood

Living and representing Christ for months in a Third-World nation or a tough U.S. neighborhood might be the greatest challenge an emerging adult ever has faced. Such a stretching experience can accelerate development toward adulthood. Few doubt that high school graduates need a challenge. Tim Elmore, who extensively researches emerging adults, reports:

> [Emerging adults] may love the exhilaration of bungee jumping and the reckless thrill of whitewater rafting, but they don't know how to negotiate adversity in the real world. . . . Much of their time is spent in a protected, failure-proof environment in which they're never given the chance to lose. Their entire lives have been full of safety devices, and they have been discouraged from going anywhere alone. . . . Healthy risk is a part of growing up. Being perennially protected and provided for not only tends to foster a prolonged childhood; it also nurtures a sense of entitlement.[2]

Derek Melleby, at The Center for Parent and Youth Understanding, gives full attention to the issue of transitions from the teenage years to adulthood. He says: "Put simply, my hope has been to offer students a vision for how to make the most of their college experience from a Christian perspective. As I've traveled the country talking to students, parents, youth pastors and college professors, I have begun to hone in on some answers and draw some conclusions. One of my conclusions is that students should strongly consider taking a gap year."[3]

Very little growth flows from days of ease. Elmore notes:

> The great goal of becoming what one is capable of becoming can be achieved only by those willing to pay the price and the price always involves sacrifice, discomfort, unpleasantness, and, yes, even pain. . . . I believe we must challenge young people to take on an opportunity that seems far bigger than they are—one that is very important and almost impossible. No doubt

they'll need encouragement and insight along the way, but nothing shatters arrogance better than a project that's bigger than the one in charge of it.[4]

Church attendance among high school seniors falls precipitously during the final months before graduation. Preparation for a missions adventure soon after high school could become an exciting, energizing focus for one's senior year at church.

Leaders could introduce the year by asking new seniors questions similar to:

- Are you fully prepared to share Christ in a clear way with any person you meet on your trip?

- Do you feel competent to answer many of the tough questions people may have about the Bible?

- Are you so consistent in your morning worship and Bible study that Christ sustains you during lonely or difficult days away?

Seniors recognizing they need much training before going out to a challenging assignment may remain active through graduation and beyond. Such faithfulness likely will lead to accelerated spiritual growth.

Sharpened Life Focus

The challenge of a gap-year mission trip can accelerate growth toward adulthood. That same experience also can help an emerging adult clarify directions for the future.

Some 18- and 19-year-olds are not ready for their freshman year of classes. They may lack the spiritual maturity to prosper in a college environment. Or they may lack any clear sense of life or vocational direction. Consequently, some may waste thousands of family dollars spent on freshman tuition. If secular universities believe they are going to get more mature and more focused students after a gap year, perhaps this could be even truer for students who return from walking with Christ in powerful ways for months.

Gap-year researchers Lark Haigler and Rae Nelson report:

> According to the American College Testing service, less than half of those entering traditional four-year colleges after high school will have graduated after five years. One-quarter will have dropped out during their freshman year. Of those in college, many will report that they do not know why they are there or how their classes relate to any life or career goal. Many of those in school, as well as those who have left, will have accumulated considerable debt without a realistic chance of finding a job. . . .

> For a number of students, a gap-year plan may make the difference between graduating successfully from college with a strategy for life beyond and floating uncertainly on a path of young adulthood that may be accompanied by significant financial and emotional costs. Through the gap year, for the first time in their highly structured lives, students may have the opportunity to discover and follow their passion.[5]

According to *The Princeton Review*:

> Likes and dislikes, plans for the future, and even the reason why you want to be in school can come into sharper focus with a simple change in environment. Time off can give students added focus and enthusiasm when they return to school. If a student isn't ready for college, time off can cultivate maturity and self- discipline. . . . Admissions counselors at professional schools tell us that taking time off for school is rarely a disadvantage for an applicant. In fact, they often choose the student who took a year off and is ready to become fully engaged in school over the one who has been on autopilot and will burn out in a few months.[6]

A gap-year mission trip also can sharpen the development of adult priorities and values. Tim Elmore notes: "Adolescents who experience premature affluence (that is, they have too many possessions and too much money) fail to develop key components that lead to healthy maturity. In short, they can remain self-absorbed and childish. To foster authentic maturity, adults must cultivate a spirit of service in young adults. Maturity occurs when people take their eyes off themselves and learn to care and sacrifice for others."[7]

Parents will know values are changing when they get an e-mail that says: "Daddy, I held a baby while she died last night. I cried a long time because this is so needless. If believers just sent a little money, we could dig a water well, and the dying would stop." Or, "All the people crowding around our van wanted Bibles. But I ran out before most got one. When I get home, I want to live more simply so I can give more."

Kingdom Impact

A gap-year mission trip can accelerate the growth of an emerging adult. But at the same time, the Spirit can move through the young adult to impact the world. Young generations always have had world impact.

Billy Graham reports that:

> Young people have been used both to save and destroy nations. Adolph Hitler built his new Germany on a foundation of teen-age Nazis by capturing the hearts of young people with his "strength through joy" program. China's Red Guard, mostly teen-agers, turned China upside down. Castro was able to seize the imagination of Cuban youth and lead them into a revolution. . . . One thing is certain: Young people today are searching for individual identity; for a challenge and a faith. Whoever captures their imagination will change the world.[8]

David Howard reports that "the history of the modern missionary movement shows that students have played a decisive role in most, if not all, of the great forward movements of the church in world evangelism."[9] The first wave of students who went out about two hundred years ago ultimately reached the coastlines of the globe's continents. A large part of that wave can be traced to a handful of students who got a vision for the nations while praying under a haystack during a rainstorm. Later they went on to form America's first Protestant missionary society.

About one hundred years later, a second wave of students surged upon the inland regions of every continent. The Student Volunteer Movement led the way in that second wave. More than 20,000 students actually went to unevangelized areas of the world to share His love and truth.

Today the Spirit may call out a final wave of students to lead the way in reaching the remaining unreached people groups. Could your teenager's generation be part of that wave?

Though recent high school graduates need leaders to guide them in strategy, they can be effective in sharing Christ. They tend to share their faith without fear. In almost every region of the world, people are fascinated with American students and are motivated to talk with them. They find students far less intimidating than older adults who share their faith. The proliferation of students on gap-year missions adventures in the U.S. and worldwide could result in immediate increases in people coming to know Christ.

Funding

Currently students can sell candy in the church lobby or write support letters to fund ten-day mission trips. Such plans may be inadequate for raising the $5,000–$20,000 that might be needed for longer missions adventures. Family savings seem to be the only viable plan.

Parents who open a missions savings account early in the life of a child will find it easier to have adequate funds. But even families who begin saving during high school may be pleasantly surprised at the number of relatives and friends who want to ensure that savings are adequate. Grandfather might say to the family gathered at Christmas: "You know we are going to sell this big house to move into something more manageable. We think there might be some funds left over when we do. For all you children with missions savings accounts, we want to add $1,000 to each so we can be a part of what you do for the kingdom someday."

High school students themselves should join parents, relatives, and church members in contributing to a gap-year savings account. The trip will capture teenagers' hearts more if they have made sacrificial contributions. Elmore notes that the discipline of saving will also accelerate growth toward maturity. "Encourage them to save, or earn the money it will take to reach the objective. Work with them to set incremental goals (if this is appropriate) to pace their spending and plan toward each step of the way. . . . Nothing feels better than to set and accomplish a worthwhile goal, especially when it involves money. This kind of experience builds the capacity for long-term commitment and helps kids nurture the important ability to delay gratification."[10]

A gap-year trip can impact how the entire family handles some of their funds into the future. Parents who experience the thrill of their own children serving alongside missions organizations will always have more interest in the financial support of those ministries. Also, the high school graduates who have seen God at work in North American and international missions always will have a bond with those movements. Those bonds can lead to missions giving for a lifetime.

Conclusion

Today students leaving the church after high school is a crisis. But if families and churches send out students on the greatest and hardest challenge of their young lives, and they see Christ at work with their own eyes, and they rub shoulders with great Christian missionaries and leaders, losing them when they get home does not seem likely.

Longer mission trips allow students to build deep relationships with people. They can experience firsthand the suffering some believers willingly accept for Christ's name. They can see how crushing poverty affects the daily lives of those they have come to love. They can learn, perhaps for the first time, what it means to join Christ in His sufferings.

Students returning home also may have a different perspective on life's purpose. They may choose to live as missionaries wherever life takes them. Those who have invested in a "mission field" are much more likely to view their own neighborhoods and workplaces as fields ripe for harvest.

Travel and living in hard places involves risk. But risk must be evaluated only after struggling with two central questions.

- What is my primary goal in parenting?
- What is my child's primary reason for being on earth?

Are you prepared to declare to your children:

> I declare you belong to Christ the King.
> If you and I both come to believe Christ is calling you
> to do something that involves risk, I will teach you
> all I know about how to live wisely and safely. I will pray

for God's wisdom and protection as you journey far from home.
At the same time,
I will do nothing to stand in your way of following
Christ's call, no matter what the risk.

CHAPTER 10: PARTNERING WITH YOUR CHURCH

Richard Ross

Your linking arms with your church's youth ministry offers the best opportunity to accelerate your teenager toward adulthood.

Leadership Roles at Church

Having leadership roles accelerates a teenager's growth toward adulthood. This fact can motivate parents and leaders to gently open more leadership roles for teenagers at church.

Your church probably tries to build its practices on Scripture. Can you think of any biblical reason for making teenagers wait years for appropriate leadership in the congregation?

Youth ministry expert Dave Rahn points out that "the Bible teaches that every believer has been given gifts to be used on behalf of the church (Romans 14; 1 Corinthians 12-14; Ephesians 4). The Bible does not teach that such gifts and resulting service are hidden like time- release capsules in the lives of Christians—inoperable until they reach the age of 20 (or 40!). At the very least this suggests that we must begin early (in youth ministry), to help identify, nurture, foster, and utilize the gifts God has given the young in the church."[1]

Veteran youth leaders Jim Burns and Mike DeVries add: "Students need to see that they're not the church of tomorrow; rather, their gifts, abilities and services are needed today. We must do everything we can to assimilate students into the life of the church. Looking back, youth ministry in the past has been far too isolated from the big church."[2]

Possible leadership roles vary by church, but they may include such things as:

- Teenagers taking public roles in worship leadership.

- Teenagers actively participating in meetings where church business is conducted.

- Teenagers serving on boards, committees, and church ministry teams.

- Teenagers leading Bible classes for children.

Equipping and releasing teenagers to lead is so valuable that every teenager needs that experience. Every teenager. Burns and DeVries believe: "Ministry and leadership are not just for the all-stars. Our calling is to help every student have an opportunity in which he or she can serve and experience the joy of ministry."[3]

If the church only plans to train the all-stars to be leaders, the youth minister can probably handle that alone. But if the mission is to equip every teenager to fulfill his or her calling, many more parents and other adults need to be involved. Dave Rahn calls for "every student leader to have the benefit of an adult partner/mentor/friend to walk with in this ministry. This is the best of all worlds—mature adult leadership encouraging, equipping, and ultimately validating student leadership."[4]

A mentor might use the following approach with a teenager who is learning how to lead:

1. I do it, and you watch.

2. I do it, and you assist.

3. You do it, and I assist.

4. You do it, and I do something else.

New leadership roles can place teenagers in relationship with adults rather than just peers. Historically, teenagers have learned to be adults by observing adults—not people their own age.

Tim Elmore reports that one hundred years ago most teenagers "acquired life skills through apprenticeships that enabled them to connect with adults in the early to middle teens, and many more 'apprenticed' by working side by side with their parents. All their lives they were connected to adults, and the jump from childhood to adulthood wasn't a challenge."[5]

Noted researcher Robert Epstein reports, "We know from extensive research both in the U.S. and elsewhere that when we treat teens like adults, they almost immediately rise to the challenge."[6]

Teenagers who serve in leadership roles move more quickly toward adulthood. But that does not mean churches have given them permission to be in those roles. That permission may require change.

Leading a church to change is somewhat like turning an aircraft carrier. Sharp turns are not practical. Trying to force God's people to make immediate changes causes conflict, damages the church, and does not help teenagers. Parents and leaders need to develop a prayer- saturated, long-term plan for gently leading a church to open new leadership roles to a young generation.

Challenging Experiences

Developmentally, teenagers are ready for challenges. That is good news, since challenges tend to accelerate teenagers moving toward adulthood. But today most teenagers fail to find much challenge at church or home.

Researcher Tim Elmore reports: "Our message to [the young] has been more about safety and maintenance than about adventure and calling. We have been protecting them rather than preparing them and coddling them instead of calling them out—challenging them to seize opportunities and make a significant contribution."[7]

Researchers Joseph and Claudia Worrell Allen add:

> For our teens, we've defined nurturance largely in terms of the things we can do for them, the stuff we can buy them, and the experiences and opportunities we can provide. . . . While young children need a great deal of parental nurturance in the form of direct assistance geared toward meeting their needs, adolescents need something different. Unlike children, teens' bodies and brains most need us to nurture and develop capacities to function on their own in this world. This means expecting things of them, not just giving things to them.[8]

Boys especially crave challenge and adventure. They pay a price when both are absent. Elmore has researched the fact that many young men are failing to move forward into adult roles. He reports: "Many male college students demonstrate the following symptoms of living in their own Neverland:

- "They are demotivated and lack the desire to assume responsibility.

- "They are disengaged from student activities or leadership on campus.

- "They return home after they are finished with college.

- "They can resort to antisocial behavior if they're deficient in social capital.

- "They lack direction and tend to postpone plans for the future."[9]

Boys are struggling for many reasons, and the solutions are complex. But one practical and powerful solution involves giving boys positive ways to experience genuine challenge. Parents and church leaders can partner to create many challenging experiences for both boys and girls.

- Teenagers can find joy and can enjoy relationships in the midst of doing hard, challenging work for the kingdom.

- They can take Christ to hard places in the local area, in the U.S., and around the world.

- They can care for those with profound needs.

- They can make significant sacrifices to see Christ's kingdom come on earth.

Teenagers might spend a Saturday morning raking leaves for church members. Or they might spend that same time rebuilding a small playground in an inner-city neighborhood. A youth minister under time pressures might have the minutes to plan the first project. But you and a group of parents assisting the youth minister might have time to create a project as challenging as the second one.

Both projects noted above are kingdom activity. But the second project has the additional advantage of moving teenagers, especially boys, toward adulthood. Challenging, hands-on experience actually impacts the development of the teenage brain (the prefrontal cortex). The developing brain needs challenging, real-world experiences balanced with a degree of supervision.

The gap-year mission trips discussed in chapter 8 may provide the most challenging experience teenage believers will ever have. Such trips primarily serve to give every person on the planet an opportunity to hear the gospel. But they also can help turn boys and girls into young men and young women.

Parents with high school students today can make sacrifices in order to save funds toward a mission trip that will last weeks or months. Parents make similar sacrifices when the high school band has an opportunity to march at Macy's Thanksgiving Day Parade or the high school French Club makes a trip to Paris.

At the same time, churches can lay the groundwork now for families that will send out teenagers in 18 years. Wise pastors might present a small check to parents during family/baby dedication. He might say, "We, your church family, want to be the first to contribute to your son/daughter's future gap-year mission trip. We invite you to go to your bank tomorrow and use this check to open a savings account for that purpose. Then, as Christ leads, we invite you to contribute monthly to that account for the next 18 years or so. Other relatives and believers likely will make contributions as well. Then, when the Spirit tells your child it is time to go, funding will be in place for this grand adventure."

Intergenerational Relationships

Writing in the *Scientific American*, researcher Robert Epstein reports, "Today, with teens trapped in the frivolous world of peer culture, they learn virtually everything they know from one another rather than from the people they are about to become. Isolated from adults and wrongly treated like children, it is no wonder that some teens behave, by adult standards, recklessly or irresponsibly."[10]

University of North Carolina professor Dr. Mel Levine asks: "How can you emerge as a productive adult when you've hardly ever cared to observe one very closely? How can you preview and prepare for grown-up life when you keep modeling yourself after other kids?"[11]

Adults who hire teenage workers have to focus on productivity. Schoolteachers have large numbers of students and are required to stay focused on content. The church is one of the only places where teenagers could build long-term relationships with those of other generations.

Researcher David Kinnaman notes: "The Christian community is one of the few places on earth where those who represent the full scope of human life, literally from the cradle to the grave, come together with a singular motive and mission. . . . Flourishing intergenerational relationships should distinguish the church from other cultural institutions."[12]

Unfortunately, adults and teenagers who attend church together have not formed many of those relationships. After conducting the National Study of Youth and Religion, lead researcher Christian Smith concluded: "Teenagers .

. . are structurally disconnected from the adult world. . . . But in terms of the implications of our work for churches, the two key words are engagement and relationships. It can't just be programs or classes. . . . Real change happens in relationships, and that takes active engagement."[13]

Teenagers need many relationships with adults to successfully become adults. The church is an ideal place for teenagers to find adult relationships. But are teenagers open to such relationships? Based on his research, Christian Smith concludes that "most teens appreciate their relationships with adults and most of those who lack them wish they had such ties."[14]

When healthy adults at church do take the initiative and form warm relationships with teenagers, good things happen. Dave Rahn reports: "When responsible adult leaders enter into the lives of students, they can help students take initial steps toward new levels of responsibility and self-reliance. Because the chief way students learn is through modeling others (usually Christian adults), it's important that adults are caring enough to inspire and show the way for students."[15]

Researcher Chap Clark summarizes the issue when he says: "A popular myth . . . is the idea of a single role model. . . . One fan, even a great one, is not enough. Every adult must attempt to add to the cumulative message of protection, nurture, warmth, and affection. . . . By far the best way to help our young is by being a chorus of support and a choir of commitment."[16]

You likely appreciate and support anything the church staff does to create intergenerational relationships for teenagers. But you should not sit back and leave that entirely to others. When you and your teenager see a healthy adult that might provide a positive relationship, you two should take the initiative and move toward that person.

Research suggests that for teenagers to grow and prosper, they need relationships with at least five significant adults.[17] Teenagers fortunate to have godly parents need a minimum of three other adults with whom they share heart connections. Heart connections are strong relationship bonds that have the potential to shape a young life.

To qualify as having a heart connection, adults must:

- Understand some of a teenager's personality, thoughts, and dreams.

- Bless and support some of a teenager's outer world and interests.

- Know and understand a teenager's family.

- Offer grace, encouragement, and unconditional love.

Church and Home

Teenagers with parents committed to their well-being have advantages as they move toward adulthood. Teenagers in churches committed to them also have advantages. But when church and home link arms in mutual support, teenagers are the most likely to prosper as adults with a lifetime faith.

Family life expert Tim Kimmel says, "The goal of the church's family ministry is to connect to the heart of each individual family leader in such a way that it better prepares those parents to develop a heart connection to their kids that subsequently inclines those kids towards a deeper love for the Lord and kindness toward others."[18]

You can look to your church to equip, support, and encourage you in your parenting role.

You can:

- Support and participate in church training events that equip you to parent your children.

- Support and participate in church training events that prepare you to spiritually lead at home.

- Support and participate in events planned for families that focus on worship, discipleship, missions, relationships, and recreation.

- Use resources the church provides for family worship, family discipleship, and preparation for adulthood.

- Participate in biblically sound counseling provided inside and outside the church during times of crisis.

Senior pastors, youth ministers, and other church leaders increasingly are spending time providing support for the home and championing parents as primary spiritual leaders. You should be sensitive to the fact that these new efforts come on top of already packed workweeks. Leaders who add workload to already overextended schedules could experience burnout. You might ask yourself and other church members:

- If we want to see one of our leaders add strong support for families to his or her job description, should we also take something off the list?

- Are there ways we can assist a leader with other duties in order to give that leader time to give new support to families?

- Is it time to consider adding an intern or associate to free up a leader to give new attention to families?

- If a leader is taking on additional duties and new areas of oversight, do we need to reevaluate compensation?

Parents and Youth Ministry

Wise youth ministers:

- Support parents and speak well of parents in every conversation and public statement.

- Tell teenagers that believing parents are to be their most important spiritual leaders.

- Stand with parents during periods of family celebration and family suffering.

- Make parents welcomed guests at every youth ministry function.

- Provide events that are targeted to the family.

- Assist in equipping parents as parents and as spiritual leaders.

- Provide resources for parents.

At the same time, you can provide practical support for the church's youth ministry. Even though you know you carry the most influence, you still can highly value the impact youth ministry makes on your offspring.

Christian Smith and his team conducted the most extensive study of church youth in history. Using the vocabulary of a researcher, Christian Smith concluded about that study:

It appears that the greater the supply of religiously grounded relationships, activities, programs, opportunities, and challenges available to teenagers, other things being equal, the more likely teenagers will be religiously engaged and invested. Religious congregations that prioritize ministry to youth and support for parents, invest in trained and skilled youth group leaders, and make serious efforts to engage and teach adolescents seem much more likely to draw youth into their religious lives and to foster religious and spiritual maturity in their young members. [19]

In other words, youth ministry makes a difference. It accelerates the growth of teenagers toward adulthood and toward a vibrant, lifetime faith. That is why youth ministry is valuable to you.

You will be wise to:

- Stay knowledgeable about what is being taught at church so you can reinforce those teachings at home.

- Speak positively to your children about the youth minister and other church leaders.

- Give positive words of encouragement and support to leaders.

- Correct inaccurate information being circulated among parents or teenagers.

- Reach out to fringe parents who are not connected to the church's youth ministry.

- Offer your home and vehicles for youth ministry.

- Offer to wait with teenagers for the last parents to arrive, so the youth minister can go home to family.

- Adjust family schedules to allow your children to be faithful to ministry events.

- Attend information meetings so you can be knowledgeable about coming plans.

- Invite teenagers who attend church alone to participate with your family in family events.

Connecting church and home is a brilliant strategy. When you and the youth leaders link arms and support one another, you likely will see teenagers become adults:

- Who love God with all their being.

- Who believe they exist for His eternal glory.

- Who invite the glorious King of kings to live His holy life through them daily, to see His kingdom come on earth.

- Who, in the power of the Spirit, spend a lifetime embracing the full majesty of the Son and join Him in making disciples among all peoples.

Parent Covenant

Does the following express your sentiments?

1. I will love God with all my heart, soul, mind, and strength. I will embrace the depth of the Father's love toward me and will experience lifetime gratitude for the grace that has been extended to me.

2. I will love others as myself.

3. In the power of the Spirit, I will embrace the majestic lordship of Christ and will join Him in bringing His kingdom on earth—for the glory of God.

4. As my second highest priority, in the power of the Spirit and with the wisdom of Christ, I will seek to rear offspring who do the same.

5. I will pray with my family daily.

6. As directed by the Spirit, I will worship with my family at home on a regular basis.

7. As directed by the Spirit, I will lead my family to serve others in the name of Christ and take the gospel to our neighborhood and world.

8. I will create for my offspring a memorable experience that will mark their transition from childhood to young adulthood. After that experience, I will

view and respond to my offspring as maturing young adults. I will lead my church to do the same.

9. I will disciple my offspring as I model life, as we "walk in the way," and through a prepared session each week.

10. I will plan times each week to teach my children what they need to know to be adults.

11. I will use Saturdays and other times to give my children a strong work ethic, to serve others and our family, and to explore and prepare for a vocation.

12. I will embrace the mentoring my church can give me as a disciple and as one called on to disciple my offspring. I will vigorously support my church as the church partners with me in preparing my offspring for adulthood and for a lifetime faith.

13. Though I will love and respect parents outside the faith, I will choose to lead my family in ways often different from them. At times this will require me to forgo good things in order to lead my family toward the best things.

14. Though the culture pressures me to believe life mostly is about me, I will choose to make life about Christ, then about my family and the kingdom, and only about me when those priorities are in place. I am on earth to bring great glory to Christ and to count all other things as loss for His surpassing greatness.

APPENDIX: LEARNING FOR LIFE MODULES

Scan the following topics as you choose teaching topics to use with your teenager.

If you want a prepared teaching module on a particular subject, go to *www.richardaross.com/learning.*

If you are willing to share one of your teaching plans with other families, go to *www.richardaross.com/learning* for instructions on uploading it.

Monday Night Topics

Identity in Christ
Purpose of Life
How to Interpret Scripture
Learning to Pray
How to Share your Faith
Service
Worship
Total Stewardship
The Trinity
The Bible
Creation and Providence
Humanity and Sin
Jesus Christ
The Holy Spirit
Salvation
The Christian Life
The End of Time
The Church
The Great Commission
Missional Living

Biblical Worldview
Apologetics
Discovering your Spiritual Gifts
Using your Spiritual Gifts
Moral Decision-Making
Dealing with Spiritual Warfare
Suffering and the Goodness of God
Personal Worship
Discerning God's Will

Tuesday/Thursday Night Topics

Choosing a Mate or Call to Singlehood

Biblical Principles
Your List of Qualities
Dating/Courting—Plan of Action
Expressing Physical Attraction
Engagement

Marriage

Biblical Roles of Husbands/Wives
Resolving Conflict
Divorce and Lifetime Marriage
Love and Respect
Using Your Marriage to Model Dating/Courting
The First Year of Marriage—Others First
Role of Premarital Counseling

Pregnancy and Childbirth

Sanctity of Life
Conception

Fetal Development
Contraception
Birth Process
Maternity Floor Field Trip

Parenting

Ultimate Purpose of Parenting
Communication
The Blessing
Discipline
Spiritual Leadership of Children
Hobbies/Extracurricular Decision Making
Grandparents and Extended Family

Family Finances

Tithing
Balancing a Bank Account
Creating a Budget
Living within a Budget
Good and Bad Debt
Credit Ratings
Insurance—Reasons and Types
Investments
Taxes
Finding Cost Savings

Maintaining a Place to Live

Mortgages
Property Taxes
Home Owners and Renters Insurance
Appliances
Electrical Systems
Plumbing Systems
Heat and Air Systems

Roof, Walls, and Foundations
Codes and Building Permits
Remodeling
Home Inspections
Neighborhood Associations and Fees

Maintaining a Car

Car Insurance
License, Tags, and Inspections
Emergencies
Choosing a Repair Shop
Scheduled Maintenance
When Your Car Breaks Down
Buying a Car
Renting a Car

Apparel

Doing Laundry
Repairing Clothes
Finding Bargains on Clothes
Appropriate and Modest Clothing
Packing for a Trip

Personal Health

Insurance
Diet and Nutrition
Exercise
When to Go to the Hospital
Choosing Health Care Professionals
Daily Personal Habits

Human Relationships

Adult Friendships

Conflict Resolution
Carrying on a Conversation with a Stranger
Relating to the Opposite Sex
Communication
Technology and Relationships
Manners and Etiquette
Dealing with Difficult People
Leadership of Peers

College

Kingdom Impact on Campus
Study Skills
How to Find a Church
How to Find an Appropriate Community on Campus
How to Approach Social Life

Civic Duties

Political Campaigns and Voting
Influencing Legislation
Participating in Politics
The Military
Local Involvement in Politics—School Board, Utility Districts

Self-Management

Choosing and Living Consistent with Priorities
Time Management
Setting Goals and Directions
Breaking Big Projects into Steps
Balancing Life
Making a Plan for Higher Education

Choosing a Vocation

Biblical Principles

God's Specific Leading
Preparing a Resume
Interview Skills
Hard Work and Integrity in Work

Your Job

Inside or Outside the Home
Relating to a Boss
Supervising Others
Adding Value to the Enterprise
Kingdom Impact in Your Workplace
Considering Promotions/Transfers

Food

Meal Planning
Special Diets
Shopping for Food
Cooking and Preparing a Meal
Serving a Meal
Basic Kitchen Skills

NOTES

Preface

1. J. J. Arnett, *Emerging Adulthood: The Winding Road from the Late Teens through the Twenties* (New York: Oxford University Press, 2004), 4.

2. Tim Elmore, *Artificial Maturity* (San Francisco: Jossey-Bass, 2012), vi.

Chapter 1

1. J. J. Arnett, *Emerging Adulthood: The Winding Road from the Late Teens through the Twenties* (New York: Oxford University Press, 2004), 4.

2. J. J. Arnett, presentation at the Emerging Adulthood Conference, Princeton Theological Seminary, 2009.

3. Robert Epstein, "The Myth of the Teenage Mind," *Scientific American*, April/May 2007.

4. Tim Elmore, presentation at Southwestern Seminary, April 6, 2013.

5. Christian Smith and Melinda Denton, *Soul Searching: The Religious and Spiritual Lives of American Teenagers* (New York: Oxford University Press, 2005), 162.

6. David Kinnaman, *You Lost Me* (Grand Rapids, MI: Baker Books, 2011), 23; and Kara Powell, Brad Griffin, and Cheryl Crawford, *Sticky Faith* (Grand Rapids, MI: Youth Specialties/ Zondervan, 2011), 15.

7. Ibid., 28.

8. Tim Elmore, *Generation iY* (Atlanta: Poet Gardner, 2010), 94. 9. Ibid., 97–98.

10. Stephenie Lievense, "The Proper Care and Feeding of Emerging Adults, Part 2," www.fyi.org, accessed July 19, 2013.

11. Ibid.

12. Tim Elmore, *Generation*, 158.

13. Ibid., 67.

14. Epstein, "The Myth."

15. Tim Elmore, *Artificial*, 50.

Chapter 2

1. www.Merriam-Webster.com/dictionary/teener.; en.allexperts. com/q/Etymology-meaning-words-1474/origin-world-teenager.htm, accessed May 23, 2013.

2. *MacMillan Dictionary for Students* (New York: MacMillan, Pan Ltd, 1981), 14, 456.

3. Don Richter, "Roots and Wings: Practicing Theology with Youth," *Agenda for Youth Ministry*, Dean Borgman and Christine Cook, eds. (London: SPCK Publishing, 1998), 134.

4. John Berard, et al., *Consuming Youth* (Grand Rapids: Zondervan, 2010), 29.

5. Ibid.

6. MacArthur Foundation Project, Transitions to Adulthood, http:// homepages.wmich. edu/~tarbuxg/washingtonpost_com%20 adolescence%20not%20just%20for%20kids.htm, accessed May 2, 2013.

7. John Santrock, *LifeSpan Development*, 13th ed. (New York: McGraw Hill, 2011), 7, 532.

8. R. T. France, *The Gospel of Matthew: New International Commentary of the New Testament* (Grand Rapids, MI: Eerdmans, 2007), 50.

9. Ibid., 665–71.

10. Deborah Lipstadt, "The Jewish Age of Majority and Its Obligations," www.myjewishlearning. com, accessed May 7, 2013.

11. Mark Kleijwesgt, *Ancient Youth* (Amsterdam: J. C. Geiben, 1991), 317.

12. Robert Epstein, *The Case against Adolescents* (Sanger, CA: Quill Driver, 2007), 16–19.

13. Jean Liedloff, *The Continuum Concept* (Reading, MA: Perseus Books, 1977).

14. Philippe Aries, *Centuries of Childhood*, trans. Robert Baldick (New York: Vintage Books, 1962), 30, 33.

15. Ibid., 30–33.

16. Ibid., 219–20.

17. "Why Were There Children on Board?" www.imdb.com/title/ tt0311113/faq#.2.1.9, accessed May 7, 2013.

18. Kennedy Hickman, "Admiral Farragut, Hero of the Union Navy," www.About.com, accessed May 7, 2013.

19. Economic History Association, "Fertility and Mortality in the United States," eh.net/encyclopedia/article/haines.demography, accessed May 7, 2013.

20. Epstein, *Case Against*, 163–202.

21. Ibid., 34.

22. Ibid., 197.

23. Ibid.

24. Ibid, 198; Elliot S. Valenstein, *Blaming the Brain* (New York: The Free Press, 1998), 126–28.

25. Eric Courchesne, et al., "Normal Brain Development and Aging," *Radiology* 216 (2000): 672–82.

26. Robert Coles, *The Moral Life of Children* (Boston: Atlantic Monthly Press, 2000); D. Kay Johnston, "Adolescents' Solutions to Dilemmas in Fables," *Mapping the Moral Domain*, eds. Carol Gilligan, et al. (Cambridge: Harvard University Press, 1988), 49–71.

27. David Weschler, *The Measurement of Adult Intelligence*, 3rd ed. (Baltimore: Williams & Wilkins, 1944), 118; J. C. Raven, "The Comparative Assessment of Intellectual Ability," *British Journal of Psychology* 39 (1948): 12–19.

28. David Black, *The Myth of Adolescence* (Yorba Linda, CA: Davidson Press, 1999), 17.

29. Thomas Hine, *The Rise and Fall of the American Teenager* (New York: Bard Books, 1999), 9.

Chapter 3

1. Tim Elmore, *Artificial Maturity* (San Francisco: Jossey-Bass, 2012), 44.

2. www.nielson.com, accessed May 30, 2013.

3. www.webmd.com, accessed April 11, 2013.

Chapter 4

1. Walker Moore, *Rite of Passage Parenting* (Nashville: Thomas Nelson, 2007), 31.

2. Tim Elmore, *Artificial Maturity* (San Francisco: Jossey-Bass, 2012), 85.

3. Robert Epstein, *The Case against Adolescence* (Sanger, CA: Quill Driver, 2007), 75.

4. Moore, *Rite of Passage*, 12–15; Elmore, *Artificial*, 127.

5. Epstein, *Case Against*, 355.

6. Robert Epstein, "The Myth of the Teenage Mind," *Scientific American* (April/May 2007).

7. Kara Powell and Chap Clark, *Sticky Faith* (Grand Rapids: Zondervan, 2011), 65.

8. See Proverbs 22:6.

9. Moore, *Rite of Passage*, 15; Elmore, *Artificial Maturity*, 127.

10. Moore, *Rite of Passage*, 107.

11. Elmore, *Artificial Maturity*, 43–44.

12. Moore, *Rite of Passage*, 15.

13. Epstein, *Case Against*, 16.

14. Powell and Clark, *Sticky Faith*, 107.

15. Ibid., 16–17.

16. Elmore, *Artifical Maturity*, 203.

17. Moore, *Rite of Passage*, 59–64; Elmore, *Artificial Maturity*, 129.

18. Powell and Clark, *Sticky Faith*, 107.

19. Robert Lewis, *Raising a Modern Day Knight* (Carol Stream, IL: Tyndale, 2007), 70–72.

20. Moore, *Rite of Passage*, 33.

21. Lewis, *Raising a Modern Day Knight*, 99.

22. Ibid., 103.

23. Deuteronomy 6:7.

24. Moore, *Rite of Passage*, 58.

25. Powell and Clark, *Sticky Faith*, 109.

26. Tim Elmore, *Generation iY* (Atlanta: Poet Gardner, 2010), 162–65.

27. Powell and Clark, *Sticky Faith*, 108.

Chapter 5

1. Janet Adamy, "Will a Twist on an Old Vow Deliver for Domino's Pizza?" *Wall Street Journal*, December 17, 2007.

2. Jamieson Borak, "Seinfeld You Magnificent Sitcom!: Seinfeld's Impact on the Sitcom from the Minutiae to the Meta," http:// RemotelyInteresting.wordspress.com, accessed April 20, 2013.

3. Search Institute.org, accessed April 30, 2013.

4. Robert Arnott, *The Top 17 Investing Quotes of All Time*, http:// Investopedia.com, accessed April 30, 2013.

Chapter 6

1. Pat Galagan, *New Factors Compound the Growing Skills Shortage*, www.astd.org/ NR/ rdonlyres/CBAB6F0D-97FA-4B1F-920C- 6EBAF98906D1/ 0/ BridgingtheSkillsGap.pdf, accessed April 17, 2013.

2. Tim Elmore, *Artificial Maturity: Helping Kids Meet the Challenge of Becoming Authentic Adults* (San Francisco, CA: John Wiley and Sons, 2012), 236. Mihaly Csiksqentmihalyi and Barbara Schneider, *Becoming Adult: How Teenagers Prepare for the World of Work* (New York: Basic Books, 2000), 4.

3. Jeremy Staff, Angel Harris, Richardo Sabates, and Laine Briddell, "Uncertainty in Early Occupational Aspirations: Role Exploration or Aimlessness?" *Social Forces*, 89, (2010), 659–83.

4. Kate Stringer, Jennifer Kerpelman, and Vladimir Skorikov, "A Longitudinal Examination of Career Preparation and Adjustment During the Transition from High School," *Developmental Psychology* (2012), 48, 5, 1,343.

5. Bureau of Labor Statistics, www.bls.gov/tus/charts, accessed April 17, 2013.

6. S.v. *intrinsic, Merriam-Webster Dictionary*, www.merriam-webster. com, accessed April 20, 2013.

7. Doug Sherman and William Hendricks, *Your Work Matters to God* (Colorado Springs: NavPress, 1990), 77.

8. Ibid., 81.

9. Chris Knoester, "Transitions in Young Adulthood and the Relationship between Parent and Offspring Well-Being," *Social Forces*, 81, 4 (2003), 1,431–57.

10. Dan Miller, *48 Days to the Work You Love* (Nashville, TN: B&H Publishing, 2005), 38.

11. Richard Nelson Bolles, *What Color Is Your Parachute?* (Berkeley, CA: Ten Speed Press, 2008), 357.

12. Sherman and Hendricks, *Your Work Matters to God*, 84.

13. Miller, *48 Days to the Work You Love*, 39.

14. Mary Abbajay and Karen Bedell, *Young at Work: The Value of the Menial*, www.career stonegroup.com/z-media/wp-value-menial.pdf, accessed April 16, 2013.

15. Ibid.

16. AP-Viacom Survey of Youth on Education, http://surveys.ap.org/data%5CGfK%5CAP-Viacom%20Youth%20Study%20Topline_ students%20grade%20the%20schools.pdf, accessed April 18, 2013.

17. S.v. *work ethic, Merriam-Webster Dictionary*.

18. Abbajay and Bedell, *Young at Work*.

19. Joseph Allen and Claudia Worrell Allen, *Escaping the Endless Adolescence: How We Can Help Our Teenagers Grow Up before They Grow Old* (New York: Ballantine Books, 2009), 61.

20. Ibid.

21. Kate Stringer, Jennifer Kerpelman, and Vladimir Skorikov, "A Longitudinal Examination of Career Preparation and Adjustment During the Transition From High School," *Developmental Psychology* (2012), 48, 5, 1,343–54.

22. Donald O. Clifton, Edward Anderson, and Laurie A. Schreiner, *StrengthsQuest* (New York: Gallup Press, 2006).

23. Paul D. Tieger and Barbara Barron-Tieger, *Do What You Are: Discover the Perfect Career for You through the Secrets of Personality Type, 4th ed.* (New York: Little, Brown and Company, 2007), 10.

24. Vernon G. Zunker, *Career Counseling: A Holistic Approach, 7th ed.* (Belmont, CA: Thomson Brooks/Cole, 2006), 413.

25. Stringer, Kerpelman, and Skorikov, "A Longitudinal Examination of Career Preparation and Adjustment," 1,345.

26. Thom S. Rainer and Jess W. Rainer, *The Millenials: Connecting to America's Largest Generation* (Nashville, TN: B&H Publishing, 2011), 105.

27. Zunker, *Career Counseling*, 413.

Chapter 7

1. *National Survey of Family Growth*, Centers for Disease Control and Prevention, http:// www. cdc.gov/nchs/nsfg.htm, accessed July 11, 2012.

2. Glenn T. Stanton, *The Ring Makes All the Difference: The Hidden Consequences of Cohabitation and the Strong Benefits of Marriage* (Chicago: Moody Publishers, 2011), 11, and Naomi Schaefer Riley, *Til Faith Do Us Part: How Interfaith Marriage Is Transforming America* (New York: Oxford University Press, 2013), 41.

3. Stanton, *The Ring Makes All the Difference*, 46.

4. Hilary Davidson, et al., *Lost in Transition: The Dark Side of Emerging Adulthood* (New York: Oxford University Press, 2011), 193.

5. Ann Meier and Gina Allen, "Intimate Relationship Development during the Transition to Adulthood: Differences by Social Class," N*ew Directions for Child and Adolescent Development*, no. 119 (Spring 2008), 31.

6. Stanton, The Ring Makes All the Difference, 179.

7. Tyler B. Jamison and Christine M. Proulx, "Stayovers in Emerging Adulthood: Who Stays Over and Why?" *Personal Relationships*, no. 20 (2013), 157.

8. Ibid., 177.

9. Ibid.

10. J. J. Arnett, *Emerging Adulthood: The Winding Road from the Late Teens through the Twenties* (New York: Oxford University Press, 2004), 75.

11. Riley, *Til Faith Do Us Part*, 44–45.

12. J. L. Tanner, "Recentering During Emerging Adulthood: A Critical Turning Point in Life Span Development," in J. J. Arnett & J. L. Tanner (eds.), *Emerging Adults in America: Coming of Age in the 21st century* (Washington, DC: American Psychological Association, 2006), 21–55.

13. Davidson, et al., *Lost in Transition*, 154–55.

14. Arnett, *Emerging Adulthood*, 75.

15. Madison S. Carroll, et al., "Ready or Not?: Criteria for Marriage Readiness among Emerging Adults," *Journal of Adolescent Research*, no. 24 (2009), 369.

16. Tyler B. Jamison and Lawrence Ganong, "We're Not Living Together: Stayover Relationships among College-educated Emerging Adults," *The Journal of Social and Personal Relationships*, 28 (4), 2010, 553.

17. Tim Elmore, *Artificial Maturity: Helping Kids Meet the Challenge of Becoming Authentic Adults* (San Francisco: Jossey-Bass, 2012), 109.

18. Riley, *Til Faith Do Us Part*, 164; Jamison and Proulx, "Stayovers," 155–69.

19. Arnett, *Emerging Adulthood*, 174.

20. Ken Hemphill and Richard Ross, *Parenting with Kingdom Purpose* (Nashville: B&H Publishing Group, 2005), 30.

21. Rob and Amy Rienow, *Visionary Marriage* (Nashville: Randall House, 2010), 9.

22. Timothy S. Lane and Paul David Tripp, *How People Change* (Greensboro, NC: New Growth Press, 2008), 56.

23. Paul David Tripp, *Broken-Down House* (Wapwallopen, PA: Shepherd Press, 2011).

24. Andy Stanley, *iMarriage Study Guide* (Sisters, OR: Multnomah Publishers, 2006), 21.

25. Gary D. Chapman, *The 5 Love Languages: The Secret to Love That Lasts* (Chicago: Zondervan, 2010, reprint), 15; and Emerson Eggerichs, The Languages of Love and Respect: Cracking the Communication Code with Your Mate (Nashville: Thomas Nelson, 2007), 57.

26. Tripp, *What Did You Expect?*, 55.

27. Paul Tripp, *What Did You Expect? Redeeming the Realities of Marriage* (Wheaton, IL: Crossway Books, 2010), 188.

28. Ibid., 235.

29. Luke Gilkerson, "Your Brain on Porn: 5 Proven Ways Pornography Warps Your Mind and 3 Biblical Ways to Renew It," http://www. covenanteyes.com/brain-ebook, accessed May 13, 2013.

30. Walker Moore, *Rite of Passage Parenting* (Nashville: Thomas Nelson, 2007), 158.

31. Arnett, *Emerging Adulthood*, 86.

32. Davidson, et al., *Lost in Transition*, 193.

33. Ibid.

34. David Olson, Amy Olson-Sigg, and Peter J. Larson, *The Couple Checkup: Find Your Relationship Strengths* (Nashville: Thomas Nelson, 2008), 110.

35. Moore, *Rite of Passage Parenting*, 174.

36. Tripp, *What Did You Expect?*, 61.

37. Olson, et. al., *The Couple Checkup*, 44–45.

38. Henry Cloud and John Townsend, *Boundaries in Marriage* (Grand Rapids, MI: Zondervan, 1999), 10.

39. Dennis Rainey, *The Art of Marriage: Getting to the Heart of God's Design* (Little Rock, AR: FamilyLife Publishing, 2011), 7.

Chapter 8

1. Patrick Lencioni, *The Three Big Questions for a Frantic Family* (San Francisco: Jossey-Bass, 2008), 180–81.

2. Tim Kimmel, *Connecting Church and Home* (Nashville: Randall House, 2013), 75–76.

3. J. D. Greear, *Gospel: Recovering the Power that Made Christianity Revolutionary* (Nashville: B&H Publishing Group, 2011), 16–17.

4. Scot McKnight, *The Jesus Creed: Loving God, Loving Others* (Brewster, MA: Paraclete Press, 2004), 47.

5. Greear, *Gospel*, 12–13.

6. Ibid., 11–12.

7. Tim Kimmel, *Connecting Church and Home*, 33.

8. Ibid., 56.

9. Norman Wright, *Raising Kids to Love Jesus* (Ventura, CA: Regal Books, 1999), 43.

10. Quoted in ibid., 50.

11. Greear, *Gospel*, 247.

12. Timothy Keller, *Counterfeit Gods* (New York: Riverhead Books, 2009), xviii.

13. David Platt, *Radical* (Colorado Springs: Multnomah Press, 2010), 160.

14. Kenda Dean, *Almost Christian* (Oxford: Oxford University Press, 2010), 18.

15. David Kinnaman, *You Lost Me* (Grand Rapids, MI: Baker Publishing, 2011), 124.

16. Rob Rienow, *Visionary Parenting* (Nashville: Randall House, 2009), 17.

Chapter 9

1.   Wikipedia, "Gap Year," accessed May 16, 2013.

2.   Tim Elmore, *Generation iY* (Atlanta: Poet Gardener Publishing, 2010), 43.

3.   Derek Melleby, "God in the Gap Year," cpyu.org, Spring 2008, accessed May 7, 2013.

4.   Tim Elmore, *Artificial Maturity* (San Francisco: Jossey-Bass, 2012), 75, 125.

5.   Lark Haigler and Rae Nelson, *The Gap-Year Advantage: Helping Your Child Benefit from Time Off Before or During College* (New York: St. Martin's Press, 2005), Kindle chapter 1.

6.   Quoted by Derek Melleby, "God in the Gap Year."

7.   Elmore, *Artificial Maturity*, 124.

8.   Billy Graham, *The Jesus Generation* (Grand Rapids, MI: Zondervan Publishing House, 1971), i, 112–13.

9.   David M. Howard, "The Road to Urbana and Beyond," *Evangelical Missions Quarterly* 21 (1985): 6.

10. Elmore, *Artificial Maturity,* 123–24.

Chapter 10

1.   Kenda Dean, Chap Clark, and Dave Rahn, eds., *Starting Right: Thinking Theologically about Youth Ministry* (Grand Rapids, MI: Youth Specialties/Zondervan, 2001), 173.

2. Jim Burns and Mike DeVries, *The Youth Builder* (Ventura, CA: Gospel Light Publications, 2002), 138.

3. Ibid., 144.

4. Dean, Clark, and Rahn, eds., *Starting Right*, 175.

5. Tim Elmore, *Generation iY* (Atlanta, GA: Poet Gardener Publishing, 2010), 58.

6. Robert Epstein, "The Myth of the Teenage Mind," *Scientific American* (April/May 2007), 63.

7. Elmore, *Generation iY*, 158.

8. Joseph Allen and Claudia Worrell Allen, *Escaping the Endless Adolescence: How We Can Help Our Teenagers Grow Up before They Grow Old* (New York: Ballantine Books, 2009), 77.

9. Elmore, *Generation iY*, 78.

10. Epstein, "The Myth of the Teenage Mind," 63.

11. Mel Levine, *Ready or Not, Here Life Comes* (New York: Simon and Schuster, 2005), 27.

12. David Kinnaman, *You Lost Me* (Grand Rapids, MI: Baker Publishing, 2011), 203.

13. Christian Smith, "Lost in Transition," ChristianityToday.com (October 2009), accessed May 13, 2013.

14. Christian Smith and Melinda Denton, *Soul Searching: The Religious and Spiritual Lives of American Teenagers* (New York: Oxford University Press, 2005), 271.

15. Dave Rahn and Terry Linhart, *Evangelism Remixed: Empowering Students for Courageous and Contagious Faith* (Grand Rapids, MI: Youth Specialties/Zondervan, 2009), 64.

16. Chap Clark, *Hurt 2.0: Inside the World of Today's Teenagers Youth, Family, and Culture* (Grand Rapids, MI: Baker Academic, 2011), 202.

17. Merton P. Strommen and Richard A. Hardel, *Passing on the Faith: A Radical New Model for Youth and Family Ministry* (Winona, MN: Saint Mary's Press, 2000), 176.

18. Tim Kimmel, *Connecting Church and Home: A Grace-Based Partnership* (Nashville: Randall House, 2013), 23.

19. Smith and Denton, *Soul Searching*, 261–62.